I0759506

INTO THE INFERNO

INTO THE INFERNO

The Story of a B-17 Gunner over Nazi-occupied Europe

BILL IBELLE

Published in the United States of America and Great Britain in 2025 by
CASEMATE PUBLISHERS
1950 Lawrence Road, Havertown, PA 19083
and
47 Church Street, Barnsley, S70 2AS, UK

Hardback Edition: ISBN 978-1-63624-558-4
Digital Edition: ISBN 978-1-63624-559-1

A CIP record for this book is available from the British Library

Printed and bound in the United Kingdom by CPI Group (UK) Ltd, Croydon, CR0 4YY

Typeset in India by Lapiz Digital Services, Chennai.

For a complete list of Casemate titles, please contact:

CASEMATE PUBLISHERS (US)
Telephone (610) 853-9131
Fax (610) 853-9146
Email: casemate@casematepublishers.com
www.casematepublishers.com

CASEMATE PUBLISHERS (UK)
Telephone (0)1226 734350
Email: casemate@casemateuk.com
www.casemateuk.com

Cover image: B-17s in formation above the clouds. (Wikimedia Commons, USAAF Photographer Joe Harlick)

The Publisher's authorised representative in the EU for product safety is Authorised Rep Compliance Ltd., Ground Floor, 71 Lower Baggot Street, Dublin D02 P593, Ireland.
http://www.arccompliance.com

Contents

Prologue

November 19, 1944

Sighted convoy at sunrise (11 a.m.). Iceland is still closed in. Flew up 50-mile fjord at 600-foot altitude. Landed at Narssaq (Bluie West I), Greenland. Approached field between 3,000-foot mountains. Landed up hill. Barren. Plenty of icebergs. Saw Greenland icecap (glacier). Saw pill boxes. Five-and-one-half hour flight. On to Iceland as soon as possible.

They hadn't even reached the war, and already their lives were in peril.

During their night crossing of the Atlantic, the cloud cover that socked in their destination in Iceland had moved west to obscure their emergency airfield in Greenland as well. They were a rookie crew on a B-17 bomber, on their way to Italy to attack the Axis powers. But first, they had to get there.

The southwest coast of Greenland was a navigator's nightmare—a region of countless fjords that snaked into the mountains like spider cracks in a damaged windshield. Their emergency air base was hidden 50 miles up one of these fjords, but finding the right one would be a challenge under the best circumstances. They planned to locate it from 10,000 feet, where they could look down on the chaotic landscape like a map and identify the crack with the right shape and location along the shattered landmass. But the cloud cover prevented that.

As they approached Greenland, the cloud ceiling dropped to 1,000 feet and as the first light of morning seeped into the Arctic world—which happens sometime between 10 and 11 a.m. in November—they were forced to fly at just 600 feet to maintain visibility.

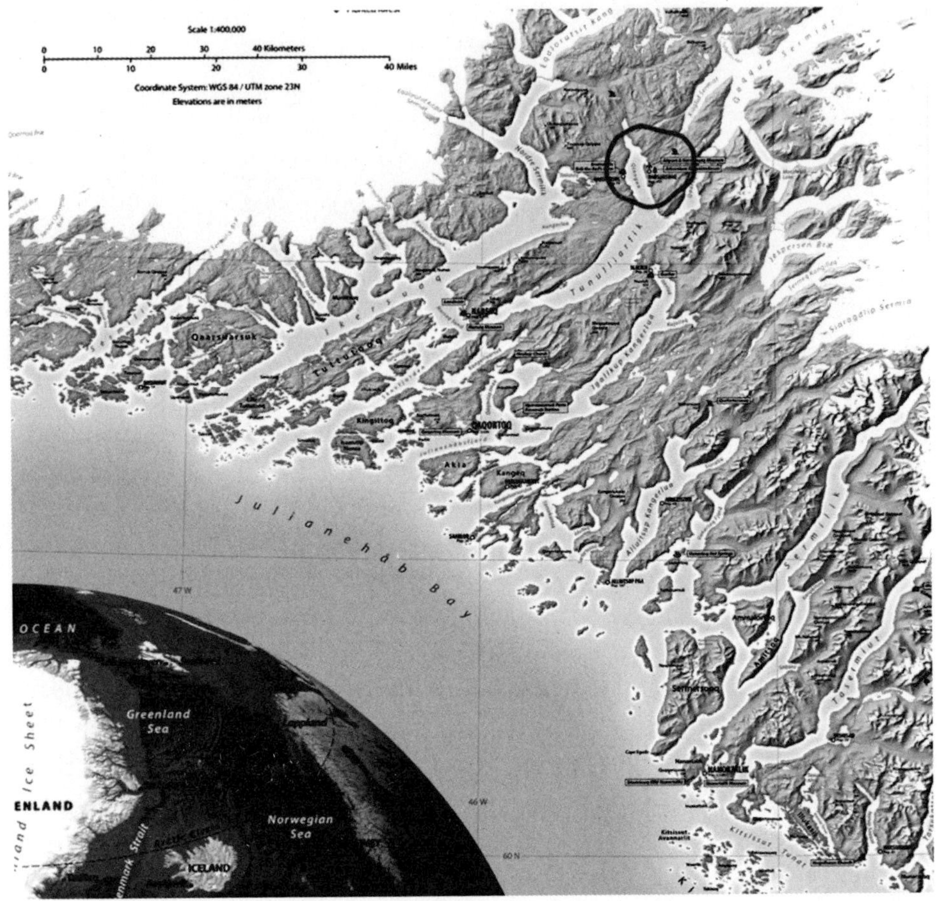

The emergency airstrip in Greenland (encircled here) was hidden among a series of deep fjords that fracture the southeastern Greenland coast. (Tom Patterson)

With the clouds hanging low over the 3,000-foot mountains, the fjords presented themselves as a series of tunnel entrances, with floors of frigid ocean and ceilings of leaden clouds. The emergency airfield was 50 miles up one of these tunnels. But which one?

Because the fjords were too narrow for the bomber to turn around, all but one of them would end in a rocky wall of death. They had no modern navigation equipment, so the navigator relied on dead reckoning—a formula of time, distance, speed, and crosswinds—to guide them across 1,000 miles of open ocean. They also had the sun and stars to help them

The Bluie West emergency airstrip in Greenland was at the end of a 50-mile fjord. The frightening airstrip was short, began at the water's edge, and ran uphill to a wall of mountains. (Mike Collins)

fix their position, but when they were forced to fly beneath the clouds, that method disappeared. The accuracy of the navigator's calculations would determine whether they selected the right tunnel, so as their plane slid between the mountain walls, the entire crew silently prayed that the navigator's calculations were correct.

For 20 excruciating minutes, they flew up the canyon. When the tunnel forked at mile 42, they exhaled in relief since this is what the correct fjord was supposed to do. The pilot banked the plane north up the left-hand fork and soon the tiny airfield appeared. It began at the ocean's edge and slanted uphill until it ended abruptly in a mountain face. In his retirement-age reflections, my father described the moment:

> Landing required almost dragging the tail wheel in the water, then rolling uphill to a stop in front of a blank wall. They had a rather well-stocked junkyard.

The danger was confirmed when they received word that a B-17 was lost over the North Atlantic on the way to Greenland and two more bombers had crashed on the Greenland icecap.

★★★

My father was a 19-year-old freshman at Dartmouth College when he was drafted and signed up for the Army Air Corps. New Hampshire was the farthest he had ever been from his home in Hartford, Connecticut. He was the first in his family to go to college and my grandfather, a car salesman with an eighth-grade education, wanted him to go to Trinity College in Hartford so he could walk to school from their apartment. Now, one year later, he was in Greenland on his way to fly bombing missions over Nazi Germany.

The crew had christened their new bomber "Mr. Bones" and painted a skeleton with a cigarette in its mouth on the nose of their plane. My father describes their plane's logo in his retirement-age reflections:

> The skeleton leans nonchalantly on a bomb, a not too subtle symbol of death. Yet Mr. Bones is also the gentle, likable end-man in a minstrel. We were nice guys, totally dedicated to our mission of the destruction of evil.

"Mr. Bones" leans casually on a bomb that is obscured in this black and white photograph. (The Ibelle family)

It was an odd sentence—the juxtaposition of the nonchalant administrator of death with the phrase "we were nice guys." To me, it sounded like a plea to the reader, as if the subtext was "Don't judge us harshly … we did what had to be done."

But, as I would learn in the process of writing this, my interpretation of that sentence was the projection of a Vietnam-era son, who was skeptical of war and the unquestioned moral correctness of our nation. It couldn't have been further from the meaning intended by men—boys really—whose attitude toward war was forged in a different era.

★★★

My father was the same age as I am now when he pulled his army-issue war diary from a box in the attic and began to elaborate on the telegram-style entries he made nearly a half-century earlier. When he presented me with the 282-page manuscript, I read it eagerly.

I can't lie. I was disappointed.

My father was not an introspective man—a fact that always perplexed me, given that he spent his professional life as a clinical psychologist. He maintained a clear line between his work as a psychologist and his family life, much as he did between his adult life and the war. So he told funny stories about his war exploits but never talked about the fighting itself, or his feelings about it. I was in my mid-40s when I first read his manuscript and wanted to know more about the emotional impact of what must have been one of the foundational experiences of his life. I was hoping for a window into my father's soul.

But the window wasn't there. The manuscript devotes more attention to how they constructed a stove from scrap metal to keep their tent warm than it does to the airmen who went down in flames around them or the destruction caused by the payload of bombs they dropped on every mission.

Perplexed and a little frustrated by this, I interviewed my father some months later about the war. I was a mid-career journalist at the time, and that morning I had interviewed the mayor of New Bedford, Massachusetts, in hopes of finding some material for my Sunday column. About halfway through our conversation, she mentioned that she had tickets to fly on a WWII-era plane from Cape Cod to New Bedford. When I asked her what kind of plane, she said, "I don't know anything about planes," and reached across her desk for the invitation.

"It's some kind of bomber—a B-17 it says."

I couldn't hide my excitement.

"My father flew on B-17s during the war," I blurted.

"You can have my ticket," she said. "I hate to fly. I can have my driver bring you down to The Cape."

The author standing in front of the B-17 "Nine-0-Nine" minutes before flying from Hyannis to New Bedford, Massachusetts, in August 1992. (The Ibelle family)

Two hours later, I was standing on the tarmac in Hyannis as the pilot fired up the engines. There was a deep bass "Cah-chug" followed by a burst of smoke; then another, and another, in quickening succession as the propeller struggled into action. The tiny explosions built into the distinctive roar of a mid-century bomber engine and the spinning propellers became invisible, creating a slight blur in front of the aircraft's enormous wings. As the oily exhaust from the four engines blew across the runway, I was engulfed in the smell that, for my father, marked the start of every mission.

I flew in my father's right waist gunner position. From his perspective, the fuselage was a metal tube, barely more than 6 feet in diameter and 74 feet long. It was like flying inside an MRI machine. I had headroom to stand straight only when I was in the center of the tube. I tried to imagine what it was like for my father, but we were flying at a few thousand feet in mid-August; my father flew his missions at 29,000 feet in the dead of winter. At that altitude, the average temperature was 40 below zero.

That night, I called my father to tell him about my flight. What I didn't tell him was that I was taking notes for my Sunday column. I hid the fact that I was interviewing him because I was worried he wouldn't say anything insightful or interesting and I didn't want to have to explain why I didn't use any of what he told me in the column. My father was a nice guy and loved me dearly, so I'd never forgive myself if I hurt his feelings.

I tried to talk to him about the horror of war without much success. I asked him whether it was difficult to drop 5,000 pounds of explosives on a city—even in the interest of defeating true evil—knowing that many of those bombs would miss their targets and hit the homes and workplaces of civilians.

"It was the business we were in," he said. "That was the job."

I didn't get much more. My father had no conflicted feelings about this war, or if he did, he certainly wasn't going to talk about them.

When I asked him about fear, he was only slightly more expansive. "We never got used to being shot at. There were only two missions when our plane didn't get shot up pretty bad. I had planes on both sides of me blow up."

Silence.

"Were they people you knew?"

"Some of them. Surviving was just the luck of the draw."

More silence.

I was hoping he would offer something more. Maybe take the conversation to an area he was interested in talking about. But that didn't happen. Like my mother once told me, "Your father is comfortable with silence. You have to get used to that."

So I decided to broach a question that had always puzzled me.

"Did your experience in the war have anything to do with your decision to become a psychologist?"

"No, that was due to other things."

Nothing more.

And this is where I dropped the ball. The next question should have been obvious: "What other things?" But I didn't ask it. In any other interview, I would have asked that question and then dozens more. I would have followed every thread, gently but persistently, for as long as I could. But this was my father, and I feared he was beginning to sense that this wasn't just a conversation. So I darted off to more factual questions, which I knew would make us both more comfortable.

That's when my father loosened up. He described the bulky heat suits they wore to avoid freezing to death at 40 below zero, and the oxygen tanks their lives depended on at 29,000 feet.

"We had more deaths from smothering and frostbite than from enemy fire," he said.

"Smothering?"

"The condensation in your oxygen ducts would freeze up and if you didn't knock the ice out every 10 minutes, you'd suffocate. When you start to lose oxygen, some guys got kind of high. They'd forget to clear their ducts and [then they'd] suffocate."

I may not have gotten what I was looking for, but I did get plenty of material for the column. My father was willing to talk about the facts—and maybe with time, he would feel more comfortable venturing into the parts I was most interested in.

So I came up with a plan. I would interview him and use those interviews to add a third piece to his manuscript. Each entry would begin with his terse diary entry, followed by his retirement-age elaboration, and then I would add portions of my interviews to create the insight and reflection I so desperately sought. It was a marvelous plan. After all, I was a journalist and had spent my adult life seeking out and capturing the experience of others.

But I blew it.

I had two kids, a three-hour commute, and spent weekends coaching my kids' sports teams. I assured myself that I'd begin next week, next month, next year—then he died. It wasn't a surprise. He had been battling emphysema for years. I just couldn't muster the courage to do with my own father what I had done with countless strangers—pull up a chair, put him at ease, and gather the details needed to help others see the world from his point of view.

Now, more than a decade later, I'm the same age my father was when he sat down at his computer to begin his reflections. Like him, I am recently retired and itchy for a project. It feels risky. There are so many ways to approach this story and so much information that is lost forever. Both he and my mother are gone; the friends and family who knew him when he was younger are dead, so there's no one to answer my questions. I waited too long. So my task is to gather as many pieces of the puzzle as possible, knowing that many will never be found and the picture will remain incomplete. But even with the limitations, I am determined to assemble enough information to paint a compelling portrait of a man and the pivotal moment in our nation's history that he helped to shape.

I feel a bit like I am flying up one of those cloud-choked Greenland fjords. It is a risky mission, and as I approach the fractured landscape of my father's past, I may find that I am flying up the wrong tunnel, destined to add my project to the B-17 junkyard.

But I will say this: When I read my father's manuscript a second time, I was transfixed. Knowing what wouldn't be there, I was able to see what was.

Note to the Reader

To avoid confusion, all primary source material is signaled as follows:

- Entries from my father's war diary begin with a date which is set in bold type and are indented from both margins.
- My father's retirement-age reflections are in smaller type.
- All letters are dated and indented.

Therefore, anything in smaller type is written by my father looking back over 50 years. Any passages that begin with a date (whether set in bold type or not) were written during the war years.

CHAPTER I

The Kingdom of Loneliness

Bert Ibelle left for the war on November 12, 1944. He had been in training for a year and a half—shuttled among a dozen bases and universities from coast to coast—New Jersey, Colorado, Nevada, California, Florida—and finally, Savanah, Georgia, where they picked up their new B-17 bomber.

They took the Northern Route to Europe, leaving Savanah at 6 a.m. bound for Bangor, Maine. It was an 8-hour, 1,200-mile flight that took them right over Hartford, Connecticut, the city where he was born and raised. I never asked him what he was thinking as his hometown slid beneath them at noon, but I'm sure it included his parents, his kid sister, and "Red," the girl he was smitten with.

Mary Jane Pierce, or "Red" as Bert refers to her in his letters, was one year behind him in high school and known for her striking auburn hair. They traveled in the same group, shared the same friends, and dated from time to time. When he went off to college, he carried a flame for Red throughout his first semester at Dartmouth and it burned just as brightly during his 18 months of Army training.

But Mary Jane was in love with another young man. Bill Harney was a three-sport valedictorian at Cheshire Academy where he was president of his class and was headed for Yale. Bill's father was a judge; Bert's father was a car salesman with an eighth-grade education.

As she wrote in a letter to Bert partway through his Army training: "I still love Bill but think of you a lot. I hope and pray that we can always, always be the best of friends."

Bert was a freshman at Dartmouth College and Mary Jane was a senior in high school when Bert was drafted. (The Ibelle family)

It was the kiss of death; every guy's worst nightmare—the dreaded "nice guy" syndrome. So as Bert watched Hartford glide beneath him and disappear into the high-altitude haze, he was locked in a rivalry with another young man—and losing badly.

It's not hard to imagine the scene: They've been listening to the steady drone of the B-17 engines for six hours when Hartford comes into view. Bert looks down from his waist gunner position as the city passes beneath them. It is a Sunday afternoon, so Red is out in the city someplace, possibly on a date with Bill, who is a year younger than Bert and hasn't been called to service yet. Bert must have felt helpless, heartsick, and cursed by fate. And at that moment, these feelings were probably more powerful than any fear he may have felt about his ultimate destination.

Bert provides no hint of his thoughts that day: His diary simply says, "over Hartford about noon." In his retirement-age elaborations, he makes no mention of the moment, which is baffling to me. He does, however, make a poignant reflection about his departure from Hunter Field, in Georgia, as he left for the war:

> The control tower cleared us for takeoff, adding "Goodbye, good luck, and hurry back to Hunter." I never forgot that send-off, and when I have occasionally flown over the area and looked down on Hunter, I've silently said, "I'm here."

★★★

The crew spent the next several days in Bangor, grounded by sleet and ice. During that time, volunteers gave the departing airmen gift bags, which contained a simple item that proved to be a weapon against a formidable enemy that none of those airmen anticipated: Boredom.

> November 13, 1944
> Dear Folks:
> The volunteers visited us today and gave us each a small, green cloth bag containing a number of items they thought might be useful. This was greatly appreciated.

Upon looking back on that gift bag from the distance of retirement, he wrote:

> The donors probably never knew that the most popular items were the tiny green-covered diary from whence these entries have been taken, and a cardboard chess set with punch-out pieces. Between us, we had nine of these game boards and wore them all out before our return home in June 1945. A marathon tournament began the day we received the sets.

After being iced-in for nearly a week, they finally received clearance to fly to their next stop, a remote air base in Goose Bay, Labrador, which lies north of Newfoundland. Bert rode to Goose Bay in the bombardier's station, the all-plexiglass nose of the B-17, which provided a breathtaking 360-degree view of the world.

> The northern lights were the most spectacular I have ever seen. Brilliant reds, greens, and yellows rolled across the sky—surfing and surging—a veritable firestorm in the heavens.

The next day, he witnessed a seemingly inconsequential scene that, for some reason, made a big enough impression on him to include in his memoir.

> Goose Bay was also a place where I experienced one of my few episodes of unmitigated envy. Air Transport Command planes were constantly coming and going. Pilots would come into the operations room and invariably spot old friends. "Hey Joe. Haven't seen you in a while. Where you headed?" "Chicago, how about you?" "London. Say, I'm supposed to be in Karachi next week. See if you can get a run there. We could have a ball." My black thoughts along with my burning desire could have melted their stabilizers.

On first reading, I attributed the scene to my father's tendency to describe his past as if it were a scene from a Bing Crosby movie. I knew he could be a little corny, but why did he feel compelled to recount this simple interaction 50 years later?

One interpretation is pretty straightforward. He was on his way to war, doing his best to suppress his fear when he overheard these transport pilots talking casually about their next delivery and where they would meet for a beer. His jealousy was simple—they were flying all over the world in relative safety, while he would soon be flying directly into the jaws of the German killing machine.

It's the most straightforward explanation, but I don't think it's the right one.

My father was a fan of Hemingway and a big believer in his "iceberg theory" of writing. The theory goes something like this: The emotional power of a story comes from what you don't see—the things the author leaves out. This includes backstory, excessive exposition, and overt displays of emotion. The deeper meaning of a story should not be explicit but, instead, should shine through implicitly. Like an iceberg, the power of the story comes from the 90 percent of its mass that remains below the surface, unseen.

It's an interesting theory, but my father often took the idea too far. He left too much out, assuming the reader (or the listener) could feel the power looming below the surface. The result was often not heightened emotion, but an absence of it.

I have concluded that this short scene, which takes place in the snow-blown desolation of Goose Bay, Canada, is the tip of an iceberg, but the mass underneath is so well disguised that it is nearly impossible for the reader to discern its meaning.

The submerged portion of that iceberg revealed itself when I came across a box of wartime letters in the basement. I was struck by the difference in style and tone between the voice in those letters and his retirement-age reflections on the war. He was just a kid when he went to war—19 when he enlisted and 20 when he left for Europe. He had already spent more than a year in training and was profoundly homesick.

During high school, Bert had a group of buddies—"the frat" as they called themselves. During their first year in college, they eagerly sought news of who had enlisted, what branch of service they ended up in, and where they were posted. During their training, they were shuttled among military bases across the country, living in spartan barracks packed with strangers, and surrounded by terrain that was nothing like New England. They were homesick and their loneliness was overwhelming.

In a letter home about a year into his training, Bert writes of his brief visit to the California branch of the Ibelle family and the relief of being among people who knew him was unmistakable. A three-word phrase jumped out at me which he used to describe how he felt throughout the previous year of training—"solitude in crowds." I think it captures the feeling of the thousands of soldiers who were shuttled among lonely military bases across the country.

In this context, that corny scene in Goose Bay takes on a different meaning. At 20 years old, his letters were already peppered with references to "the good old days" of hayrides and tobogganing in Goodwin Park with Red and the gang. When he overheard those transport pilots laughing and making plans for where they would meet next, his thoughts must have turned to his hometown buddies, who he may never see again.

Within "the frat," Bert had a trio of close friends—Bob, Saul, and Fran. I had met Saul and Bob, but not Fran. I don't recall my father ever mentioning him, but then again, what kid pays attention to their parents' stories about people they've never met? They probably just drifted apart as high school friends are prone to do.

But reading through that box of letters, Fran fascinated me. His letters were so alive and his language so irreverent and similar to our own. The energy and steady flow of playful insults in those letters provided a sharp contrast to the relatively staid language of my father's letters. This is an

Bert (far left) and Fran (far right) during the summer before they went to war. In the middle are Bob and Saul. (The Ibelle family)

unfair comparison, of course, since Fran was writing to a friend and the only letters I have from my father were written to his parents.

This is another frustrating hole in this story. I have Red's letters to my father because he saved them, but none of my father's letters to her. Nor do I have any of my father's letters to his buddies. So I have no record of my father's voice when he was talking to his friends or his love interest. It's just another potential insight swallowed up by the hungry jaws of time.

Because Fran was such an avid letter writer, which was probably a measure of his own loneliness, I have at least a small sample of how these guys talked to one another. Fran was girl-crazy, profane, and entertaining. He frequently began his letters by berating my father for not writing more often. He was not alone in this criticism. Although my father was a loyal friend and devoted son, it appears that he was an inconsistent correspondent with everyone except Red.

These two themes—love and friendship—are a substantial part of the hidden mass that gives the iceberg of my father's wartime memoir its power. It was a weight I missed on the first reading of his manuscript.

I was hoping for a window into my father's soul, but my father was not capable of providing that kind of opening. At least not directly.

But it's there, floating beneath the story of these two high school friends—Fran and Bert—who fought the war on opposite sides of the globe.

This is their story.

CHAPTER 2

1943: Dear Folks

While Bert was at Dartmouth pining for the girl back home, Fran was having a grand old time during his first year at the University of Connecticut. In one letter he chews out Bert for not writing and speculates about what he's doing with his left hand at an all-men's college: "Hands off Oscar and write me a letter."

He commiserates with Bert about the grind of their first round of final exams but quickly moves on to his favorite college subject: girls. He makes no attempt to hide his unbridled glee about a couple of co-eds he's dating and signs the letter "Fran the gals' man."

A month later, Fran raves in his letter about the "snazzy blonde" he's just met. From his letters, Fran comes across as an impulsive, high-energy boy who's away from home for the first time and giddy about his newfound freedom.

> February 14, 1943
> … There's a girl down here that has my heart ticking and jumping. She isn't any dumb blonde either. In fact, she was valedictorian of West Haven High. I went out with Carol (that's her name) and we went to a show on campus and then walked all over. Gee, it was perfect out because it had snowed all day and now the trees and grounds were all covered. What a sight, what a walk, what a girl. Christ, I'm going to hate to leave her.

But leave her he would. Like a whole generation of young men, the Army yanked Fran out of college and threw him into the rigors of boot camp. For Fran, that happened in March; for Bert, the call came in April. Because they were smart and capable, the Army groomed Bert and Fran for larger responsibilities. Fran was eventually sorted into the Army Engineers while Bert entered the Army Air Corps hoping to become a pilot. Both spent more than a year moving from base to base across the country in a grueling regime of physical and academic training.

Since Fran entered the Army first, his early letters to Bert are filled with advice on what to bring—a shaving kit, shoe polish, extra underwear, and a cigarette case "because your ciggies take a beating." He also warned his buddy about the brutal conditions of boot camp, with its 14-hour days and 24-mile marches. There is so much foreshadowing in their letters that it's hard to believe it's not fiction.

> April 6, 1943
> … Boy am I tired. Especially my feet. We trained in grenade throwing today. Last week, I qualified as a marksman. Somehow, I'm getting the knack of shooting a weapon. It's going to come in handy someday, I guess.… I don't know if we will be able to see each other for a hell of a long time, so for god's sake, shake your ass and write plenty … Well Dartmouth man, if you can stay out of this thing called the Army, do it. You're not missing much.

Like many young men at the time, Bert had no interest in staying out of the Army. He wanted in. He wanted to fly. He wanted to help defeat the Nazis. So when the call came on April 23, he chose the Army Air Corps and shipped out.

> May 1, 1943
> Dear Folks:
> By the time you get this letter, I'll probably be on my way to some camp. It was tough leaving you Friday. For the first time, I knew how much you mean to me, and how much I mean to you.

Bert's introduction to the military was the polar opposite of Fran's. Rather than some isolated boot camp, he was stationed in a luxury hotel on the Boardwalk in Atlantic City, New Jersey. He spent the first month of basic training housed in the famous Hotel President, where he could spend

The postcard Bert sent to his parents showing his cushy first boot camp assignment. Things were about to change for the worse. (The Ibelle family)

his off-duty hours reading in a leather chair and listening to the sound of the ocean. In one of his early letters home, he asked his mother to send his bathing trunks.

Bert's good fortune didn't go unnoticed by Fran, who was sweating it out at Fort Leonard Wood in the Ozark region of Missouri. In his next letter to Bert, he opens with a reference to the year they were supposed to graduate from college:

> May 1, 1943
> Greetings ex '46—meet another ex '46, now a GFU (General Fuck Up): I received a letter from Mom Ibelle saying that you're generally pleased with the Army. I can see why, since you are starting your Basic in a hotel room....

As it turns out, Bert didn't need the bathing trunks. After a short stay in Atlantic City, he was transferred to a crowded barracks in the high desert east of Denver, where the nights were frigid and the days scorching hot.

Meanwhile, Fran's performance on the Army's aptitude exams earned him a spot in the Army Engineers, which delayed his deployment while he received specialized training at a series of colleges around the country. His first stop was the University of Kentucky.

It was the beginning of a seesaw ride the two buddies would continue for the rest of the war. While one was going up, the other was coming down.

> May 15, 1943
> … Tonight, I'm taking out a senior from the University of Kentucky. Ouch, my pocket is going to be one sorry sight tomorrow. But who cares, I'm going to have a good time while I can. These women out here are really beautiful, no shit. I thought Hartford had more than its share, but Lexington has it beat any old damn day. And the co-eds are something for the eye too. Man, they are nice, and the friendliest gals you ever want to meet. They don't give you the cold shoulder whenever you talk to them like our gals back home. Nope. At college dances, only the babes can cut in. And man-oh-man is that fun. I'll give you more dope on the broads once I've taken more of them out. So far I've only dated half a dozen or so, so give me time….
> Wolfingly yours, Fran.

While Fran studied engineering and dated as many co-eds as possible, Bert's day began at 3:15 a.m. and continued for more than 12 hours of drills, calisthenics, two-mile runs with packs, followed by rigorous coursework about machine guns, cannons, power turrets, bomb racks, and sights. His days of reading in a leather chair, serenaded by the pounding surf were a distant memory—and his loneliness was inescapable.

> July 17, 1943
> Dear Folks:
> Well, here I am, 2,000 miles from home somewhere outside Denver…. How about having a portrait made of the three of you [he had a little sister] like the one of grandpa and grandma Ibelle that's on the desk. I sure would like to have one because I doubt

I'll be home for quite a while and could at least have the picture to look at.... I was just thinking about where I would have been at this time last year. Probably down at the beach with Fran, Bob, Saul and some of the others. We'd be raising Cain and having a swell time. Now I'm in Colorado, Bob's in Massachusetts, Fran's in Kentucky and Saul's in Wisconsin. Boy, what change a year can make.

CHAPTER 3

Distance

I was just one year older than my father was when I, too, wrote a letter home from Colorado. Although we were both on a year-long journey around the country, our circumstances couldn't have been more different. For me, the high peaks of Colorado mirrored my soaring spirits as I explored the country in a shitbox car with no heat; for my father, that desolate airstrip in the high plains of Colorado mirrored his loneliness at a time when the things he wanted most were back home in Hartford.

My father slept in a crowded barracks full of strangers—"solitude in crowds." I traveled the country with my college roommate and when our day was done, we slept beside the car in some vast stretch of the Arizona desert or, when the opportunity presented itself, on a friend's floor. I had no girl back home to pine for and there was no place I'd rather be than on a spectacular stretch of road on my way to who-knows-where.

But the contrast didn't end there. In a few months, my father would be a member of a bomber crew flying missions over Germany; in a few months I would be a member of the Phoenix rugby team playing tournaments all over the Western states. Having just graduated from college, my only responsibility was to have fun; my father's only responsibility was to help save the world from Hitler while trying his best not to make a premature exit. For me, the 2,000 miles from Colorado to Hartford was a measure of freedom; for my father, that same 2,000 miles was a measure of loss.

Distance: It is a concept that can mean so many things depending on the context. This book is, in part, the product of a haunting distance that cannot be measured in miles. My father was a wonderful man, but there was always something that stood between us, as if there were an unseen force field that prevented intimacy. It took decades for me to realize that this force field existed and I have never found a word to describe it adequately.

Maybe it's a generational thing. My father grew up in an era when men were expected to hold their emotions close and keep any complex feelings to themselves. His generation was forged by a string of cataclysmic events—childhood during the Great Depression, adolescence during a World War, and young adulthood in the soul-crushing, homogenized culture of the 1950s. So is it any wonder that, as fathers, these men disappeared into their expected roles?

I have many friends who describe their fathers as detached in some way. For the most part, these were good men who were expected to navigate the world while wearing emotional handcuffs. I doubt they would see it this way, but from the perspective of my generation, it seems like their culture hobbled them in both friendship and family.

At times I wonder whether my kids experience me in this way. I certainly hope not. My father worked long hours, leaving for work before we got up and not returning until around 9 at night. I was also gone long before my children woke and didn't return until dinner. To make up for this weekday absence, I made it a priority to be a presence in the evening and weekend lives of my two children. I changed diapers and invented bedtime stories. I coached their teams and my wife and I spent weekends boating, skiing, and hiking with them. Their friends were a constant presence in our house and sometimes came on vacations with us. We had fun.

But still, there are times when I feel my own brand of remoteness holds me apart from those I love the most. I am, after all, my father's son. So there is a distance in me that I can't entirely overcome. My heart aches when I feel it, but it is as much a part of my inheritance as my voice, my hairline, and my integrity.

Maybe that's what this project is all about: an attempt to bridge that chasm; to close that distance—even if only a little.

CHAPTER 4

Love is Like a Rocket

When Bert received the next letter from "Fran the Gal's Man," his exuberant buddy was singing a different tune. An unexpected event had inspired him to forego the drinking and dancing in favor of reading, writing letters, and listening to the radio.

> July 5, 1943
> Hello you old cock knocker:
> … I met this beautiful co-ed when I first came here and we have been going out ever since. She went home for the summer. She lives right near Cincinnati, so I go up there every weekend and what a swell setup. I stay at her home, get my meals there, and to top it off we get the family car, a '41 Olds, for the whole weekend. Only one bad thing. We have fallen for each other in such a great way that it's going to hurt both of us when I go on my way and our love affair comes to an end for the duration. Darn, I never thought I could go gah-gah for a girl at my present age, but love's a screwy thing. It hits you like a rocket. Anyway, we have agreed that it's her for me and vice versa, but we won't make any plans until the war's over. We figure plenty may happen by then, but for now, we are having the grandest weekends we can work up. They have to be great because there are only a few left.

There was no "Wolfingly yours" at the end of this letter. The young man who made it his mission to date every co-ed at the University of Kentucky had fallen in love. In another stroke of good fortune, he was promoted to the Army Specialized Training Program (ASTP), which ensured that he would remain stateside for several more months while he received specialized training at a series of universities.

> August 4, 1943
> Dear Air Corps:
> God damn it was good to hear from you. No shit, I thought you had forgotten about me. I'm at Ohio State University now, my third college so far. I'm happy to report that I won't be going overseas for a while. You see, I have joined that goldbrick society called ASTP. Snap my balls, this setup is a farce. No shit, it just ain't the Army. I thought life in Lexington was a snap, but this has it beat by miles. Exercise, swimming, movies, drills, sports. The food is great and it's all you can eat. I'm telling you Bert, get into this setup if you can. You'll like it. It's a lot of schoolwork, but you're getting a damn good education, and when this fucking war is over, all you'll need is about a year and a half more of college for a degree. And when you're done with this course, you'll have a good shot at a non-com rating, or even a commission. I'm getting an education plus being paid.... Now peckerhead, don't get hutsy-tutsy just because I've gone gaga over a femme. If you saw her, you wouldn't blame me. No crap, she looks just like Carolyn Hill, enough said? Besides, she's worth a little dough, has a car, will get her degree next March, and loves me dearly. What the hell more do I want? God damn, I haven't seen her for two weeks now and I'm going bats.

He wrote again a month later from his new post at North Central College in Naperville, Illinois, a sleepy town that he described as having "perfect symmetry with 11 churches and 11 bars." He wrote about his heavy academic workload and chewed Bert out for not writing, saying that "a close friendship is a great thing" and that good buddies should stay in touch. But he saved his real question for his closing: "... Well jocko, give me some info on the red-haired luvva."

The red-haired luvva was driving Bert batty. Mary Jane's letters were filled with mixed messages. She had two young men battling for her affection and she was the first to admit that she was mixed up. After all

"Red" on the Flat Rocks at Old Lyme Shores where she spent hours pondering her feelings about Bert. (The Ibelle family)

she was 18 years old, just three months out of high school, and working her first job in the Finance Department at City Hall.

Unlike Fran, who could visit his love interest every weekend, Bert was at a terrible disadvantage in the romance department. Mary Jane was 2,000 miles away and had only seen him a couple of times in the last year and a half. Meanwhile, his rival was still at home and winning the battle for Mary Jane's heart. So Bert competed the only way he could—through the mail.

As I noted earlier, I have none of Bert's letters to Mary Jane, so what he said in those frequent letters has to be inferred from her responses.

> September 20, 1943
> Dear Bert:
>
> … When I read your letter, you sure got me thinking of the good old days. I don't think I'll ever forget my Junior year. It was fun. The hayride you spoke of brings back memories too. You know I was going to ask Big Ed Doyle to that, but Mae did, so I asked you. Boy, was that a good miss! I wonder if we would have gone out anymore if I hadn't missed Ed that night. Think of all the fun and good times we would have missed.

She wrote again five days later, capturing what life was like for the girls back home. Soldiers weren't the only ones overwhelmed by loneliness.

> October 25, 1943
> Dear Bert:
> I was just reading over my old letters. That's what the gals at home do during the evenings now. I was reading yours and it was really fun to look back and think of all the fun we had. The time you asked me up to Dartmouth for a weekend and the time you came home and we went to the Yale–Dartmouth game. There's no getting away from it, I certainly had some good times with you.
> You know Bert, you are about the only fellow I can write to and say anything because we have so much in common—friends, school and fun. Maybe I should let well enough alone, but I just feel like writing to you. I don't believe I have ever told you about it, but I came very near calling the whole thing off with Bill. I still don't know exactly why I didn't. I guess I'll always have a weakness for you even though I believe it's Bill. Try and figure it out if you can, but I know I can't yet.
> By the way, please don't misunderstand me Bert, I'm not trying to string you along. That isn't in my mind at all. Maybe by now you have met some girl and have forgotten me. If that has happened, or when it does, I would like very much to meet her someday.
> Love Mary Jane
> PS: Write soon, please

She thinks I'm the best … She loves Bill … She almost called it off with Bill … She believes Bill's the one … She hopes I can find another girl … Please write soon.

Despite that whiplash-inducing letter, things were looking up for Bert in other ways. He had just been accepted to Air Cadet School, and would soon transfer to the University of Nevada to learn how to fly small planes. If that went well, the army would transfer him to Santa Ana, California, where he would compete to become a bomber pilot, bombardier, or navigator.

In a letter to his parents, he apologizes for not writing more often, then describes some unnerving developments at the base.

> October 7, 1943
> Dear Folks:
> … There has been quite a bit of tough luck out here lately. A week ago Sunday, a B-24 crashed in Denver setting fire to three houses and killing a cow. Witnesses said that flames from the explosion went a thousand feet into the air. Exactly 48 hours later, another B-24 from Lowry crashed in Colorado Springs. All were killed except a gunner who managed to get out. The next day, another B-24 from the Pueblo base this time, crashed in the mountains and only the bombardier got out. Two days later, another B-24 from Lowry went down with all on board. Then things quieted down until Monday when a B-24 from the Pueblo base went down in Mississippi while on a cross-country hop and all were killed. Total: 8 days, 5 B-24s, 43 men killed and two survived. Pretty rough for one week.

I'm sure that was not the kind of news his parents were hoping for. But the danger during Bert's training year was very real. In all, more than 15,000 young men died during aircrew training during the war, according to the Army Air Forces Statistical Digest. In 1944 alone, there were 16,000 accidents, 4,600 planes wrecked, and 4,973 fatalities—all before the airmen left the country.

The reason for this mayhem was that America was in emergency mode, churning out planes and crews at an astounding rate. From 1940 to 1945, the US manufactured 300,000 planes and many of them were new designs that had never been tested. In addition, most pilots had no flying experience before they began training. The Army was cranking out pilots as fast as they cranked out planes. In 1939, fewer than 1,000 pilots graduated basic flight training, but by 1943 that figure had grown to 165,000.

Bert's transition to pre-flight training got off to an ominous start when his train encountered a blizzard on the way from Colorado to Nevada.

October 31, 1943
Dear Folks:

I'm writing this on a westbound train somewhere out of Ogden, Utah. It has been a pretty rough trip. Just outside of Ogden, we hit a herd of cows. We butchered enough to supply New York for a week. (9 cows, 3 bulls and a horse.) It took more than an hour to cut four of them out of the brakes so we could get moving again.

When he finally arrived at the University of Nevada, Bert's training began at 5 a.m. and continued to 9 p.m. The 16-hour days included a steady diet of math, physics, history, geography, and English. During breaks from classwork, the ever-efficient Army protected soldiers from the temptations of idle time with a host of creative and highly productive tasks such as weeding the grassless airfield.

Bert's next letter to his parents ended with a PS saying, "I'm glad you saw Mary Jane. I sure wish I could." And for good reason. Whenever Mary Jane expressed confusion about her love for Bill, she always concluded by telling Bert that her choice would be much clearer if she could see him again. The repeated reminders that a furlough might turn things in his favor must have been agonizing.

Conducting his amorous campaign through the mail was not easy because the Army mail was far from reliable. One fellow trainee complained to Bert that he hadn't heard from his wife in five weeks, then received eight letters from her on the same day. Several months later, when Bert was at the war in Italy, an airman in the next tent received a package from home on January 6 that had been mailed in September. "At one time it was filled with cookies, but now it's just powder and dust," Bert wrote in a letter home. A recent news story told of a letter sent by an American soldier in 1945 that was delivered in December 2021—76 years after it was mailed, according to a story in *Newsweek* magazine.*

---

* Ayumi Davis, "WWII Soldier's Letter Meant for His Mother Delivered to His Widow 76 Years Later." *Newsweek*, January 6, 2022, https://www.newsweek.com/wwii-soldiers-letter-meant-his-mother-delivered-his-widow-76-years-later-1666642.

The result was that letters frequently arrived out of sequence, which led to misunderstandings among lovers struggling to maintain a long-distance relationship.

> November 1, 1943
> Dear Bert:
> You evidently didn't receive my last letter for I tried to explain a little. No doubt, I didn't make myself too clear. The facts are these: I believe I still love Bill but still think a lot of you. To put it more clearly Bert, I could love you if it weren't for Bill. I don't know of any plainer way in which to put it. I hope that I haven't put it too bluntly.

In that same letter, she made another reference to her hope that he could find another girl, which was not the type of encouragement Bert was looking for.

> When I began to read the paragraph you wrote beginning: "You know, I met a girl some time ago and fell in love with her ..." I was sure that you had met someone down there. I really wish that you could find someone for your sake. But Bert, I hope and pray that we can always be the best of friends.

Apparently, Bert didn't receive that letter either, because Mary Jane had to write a third letter making the same point and adding a new concern: their differences in religion. Bert was Protestant and Mary Jane was Catholic. She wanted to know if he had ever considered "the complications that would arise from this."

The difference between Protestant and Catholic might not seem like a big deal these days—same God, same Trinity, same Bible—but in 1943, it was a wide chasm. Mary Jane's best friend, Rhoda, had been in a long-term relationship with the star of their high school football team, but the relationship ended when Rhoda, a Protestant, refused to raise their future children in the Catholic faith of her boyfriend. This unexpected breakup made a big impression on Mary Jane, who noted in her letter to Bert that "I would never, never give up my religion for anyone for any reason."

Bert had no intention of asking her to do that, since religion was not a big part of his identity. But it underscores the enormous frustration of trying to have the most delicate conversation of your life through the mail and having it interrupted, delayed, and delivered out of sequence. In this age of instant communication, it's virtually unimaginable.

CHAPTER 5

1944: "Screwed, Blewed, and Tattooed"

For Bert, 1944 brought a new adventure. It was time for him to learn how to fly.

His training began in a small plane and, aided by his iron stomach, he demonstrated an immediate aptitude as a pilot.

> February 14, 1944:
>
> Dear Folks:
>
> This morning, right after I called you, I went up for the first time. It was quite an experience and I don't know quite how to describe my feelings. First of all, several of the fellows had been getting quite sick on their flights, and that worried me a little, especially when the fellow ahead of me messed up things so that we had to wash the plane with a hose before I could go up.... I did several takeoffs and landings before the instructor took over and we did some spins. Boy was that fun. There's no sensation of falling at all, but you feel as though your head is slipping down over your backbone. You're so heavy that it's hard as hell to move. We also did several different kinds of stalls. Those are really fun. You go up and see nothing but sky, then all of a sudden there's the ground where the sky ought to be. Saturday was the roughest day yet, and although I wasn't supposed to fly, the instructor took me up instead of some of the other fellows, as he thought I wouldn't get sick as easy. We did a

> lot of stalls and turns and the instructor was quite amazed that I could do so well never having flown before. I'm beginning to get the feel of the plane and I'm having lots of fun.

Bert must have written similar descriptions to Mary Jane, because she was so impressed with his descriptions that she didn't wait to get home from City Hall to write back.

> March 9, 1944
> … Boy, the flying sounds exciting. It must be a wonderful feeling when you're up all alone. So peaceful. Oh gosh! I better get out of the clouds and get to work.

Bert also received some other good news: Bill had been drafted and shipped out to Texas. Mary Jane wrote that before Bill left, they had a major "misunderstanding" and she had never been so mad at anyone in her life. She said she wanted to call Bert, "but that seems just a little wrong. I wonder why of all the kids I used to know, I would think of you. I guess …"

Unfortunately, the next page of the letter is missing, so we'll never know how Mary Jane explained her urge to call Bert in her moment of crisis. Whatever the reason, by the time she sent her next letter, she had patched things up with Bill, so the window slammed shut on Bert as soon as it opened.

Mary Jane wondered in her letter whether Bert's unwavering devotion was simply nostalgia: "You've been away so darn long and I'm one of the girls you remember from the good old days." She hoped that he could find someone new and added: "You know how I feel about you without me repeating myself. You're still the tops, and if there were more like you, oh my."

Bert was getting nowhere.

Although Mary Jane's letters were a baffling bundle of mixed messages, they also reveal a thoughtful teenager who was sensitive to how the war could distort romantic feelings. Her letters are peppered with news of former classmates who were getting engaged and married to boys as they went off to war.

> April 21, 1944
> … Estelle eloped with a sailor she's known for only eight months. I certainly hope she never has cause to regret it. Maybe I'm a little backward or something, but I still think these kids are crazy. But maybe it's me who's crazy.

Mary Jane was far from crazy. The numbers tell the story: the marriage rate in the United States more than doubled when war broke out in Europe and skyrocketed another 60 percent following Pearl Harbor. Mary Jane was correct that this crisis-induced burst of hormones might end poorly. A February 3, 1946 article in the *New York Times* began with this sobering observation: "More than half of America's 1,500,000 war-wed GIs have returned. Already more than half of these 800,000 young men is entangled in divorce proceedings. Experts are predicting that by 1950, two out of three of these wartime marriages will end in divorce."*

Mary Jane may have been confused, but she had good reason not to trust romantic notions born in such an extreme crisis.

★★★

In keeping with their seesaw war experiences, Bert's rising fortunes meant that Fran's were about to plummet. By the beginning of 1944, Fran had been transferred to the University of Chicago. He raved about the food, the beds, the beauty of the school, and being "right in the midst of one of the wildest, fun-making cities in all the US." But it didn't take long for the Army to deflate Fran's boyish enthusiasm. In March, the Army abruptly closed the ASTP program and tossed him back into the dreaded infantry. He was immediately transferred from the University of Chicago to Camp White, a massive bootcamp in southwest Oregon

---

* Jere Daniel, "The Whys of War Divorces; Experts who surveyed the wreck of many soldier marriages offer six basic reasons for disaster." The *New York Times*, February 3, 1946, https://www.nytimes.com/1946/02/03/archives/the-whys-of-war-divorces-experts-who-surveyed-the-wreck-of-many.html.

known to soldiers as "the Alcatraz of training camps." In Fran's next letter to Bert, you can hear the enthusiasm splutter out of him like air from an unknotted balloon.

> March 30, 1944
> Hello you flying asshole:
> Damn, don't you ever lift that right hand of yours. Put a pen in it and let your pals know how you're making out. After all, you're the only one of the gang who has a chance of getting his wings, and hasn't been fucked royally, say like me.
> I'm back in the Army as a private and Christ, it looks as though it's going to stay that way. ASTP folded two weeks ago and all the men were immediately assigned to infantry divisions. So here I am out on the West Coast like you, about 3,400 miles from home, and soon, where we're going, it will be 3 or 4 times that much. I'm taking a refresher in basic training, then I'll be transferred to California for amphibious training, then shoo shoo baby, off to become a Jap hunter. So that's my position now: screwed, blewed, and tattooed.
> The trouble here is that the 96th is one of the most fucked up divisions in the country, more accidents here than you can shake a stick at. Popping guys off with grenades, artillery, rifles, everything. Regular members of this unit who have survived 17 months are just lucky. They're teaching us the business in two or three months. One officer said our first maneuvers will be our first time on enemy soil. If we come through alive, we passed the test.

Fran also mentioned that if his unit stayed in the States for more than a couple of months, he might "middle-aisle it with my Kentucky belle if she's willing. Damn, may as well enjoy life while you can."

Meanwhile, Bert's military prospects were on the rise. In March, the Air Corps transferred him to the Santa Ana airfield in southern California where he had a shot at becoming a pilot, bombardier, or navigator. He had been in the program for three weeks when the Army suddenly pulled the plug, just as it had on Fran. In this case, the Army decided to slash the size of its officer training program and "washed out" nearly an entire class of recruits.

March 30, 1944
Dear Folks:
I washed out on the second list. Out of the 88 fellows who went to Santa Anna with me, only 14 made it. Out of the 250 in my squadron, they classified 44 pilots, 11 navigators, and only 4 bombardiers. I had applied for bombardier.

Bert was crushed. But unlike Fran, the Army didn't throw him into the infantry. Because he had previous training as a gunner, they sent him back to Nevada, which meant he would still get to fly. He studied the mathematics of proper gun sighting and learned how to track targets with turret guns. They practiced shooting at moving targets while on the move themselves by skeet shooting with shotguns from the back of a pickup truck going 30 miles an hour. On one day, he shot 125 shotgun shells. "That's rough on the shoulder," he wrote to his parents.

His next training session was on oxygen. During bombing missions they would be flying at nearly 30,000 feet, far above the altitude that a man can survive without supplemental oxygen. The initial training was done in a pressure chamber rather than on airplanes so that trainees could practice in a controlled environment.

May 9, 1944
Dear Folks:
Our oxygen training climaxed in two trips into the pressure chamber. Our first "flight" was to 18,000 feet where we stayed for 15 minutes without oxygen. It was quite a sensation. Several of the fellows

Bert proved to be an excellent gunner and while he was flying missions over Europe, was given the added assignment of gunnery instructor to train new crews. (The Ibelle family)

> passed out, and the importance of our oxygen equipment was brought home to us. The second "flight" was to 38,000 feet where we stayed for a little over an hour, with oxygen of course. A man is supposed to be able to last about 45 seconds without his mask at that altitude. One of the fellows volunteered to take his off, and he lasted just a little more than a minute.

He added an addendum to the letter before he mailed it the next day, saying that he finally took his first flight in a B-17.

> May 9, 1944 (continued)
> ... It was really swell. The air was rough as the devil, as it always is in Nevada. It was like riding a roller coaster for 6 hours. Most of the fellows got sick as the devil.

Bert's next stop was Florida, where he would complete his bomber training at the edge of the Everglades. But first, he was granted a week-long furlough and he made a beeline to Hartford. In another stroke of good fortune, his time off overlapped by a few days with Fran's. So after 14 months of Army training, Bert saw his family, his love interest, and his best friend all during a one-week furlough. It was a feast for a starving man.

During the furlough, two members of Bert's crew took a bus from Manhattan to visit him in Hartford. Apparently the two young men—the tail gunner, Ben Lambert, and the left waist gunner, Gene Wisby—enjoyed Hartford a lot more than the Big Apple, which they found noisy and confusing. At 19 years old, Ben was the youngest member of the crew (Bert was now 20), and he had another reason to like Hartford—a certain young woman named Gerry who was a friend of Mary Jane's.

> October 15, 1944
> Dear Folks:
> ... The fellows had a swell time up in Hartford. They keep talking about the New England hospitality, Mom's cooking, and what a swell family I've got.... I didn't know it until after, but that was Ben's first date. Man, that kid's a character. He really went for Gerry in a big way. He's been in a daze ever since and he's funny as the devil. All he talks about is Hartford.

Apparently Ben was not shy about expressing his newfound affection in a flurry of letters to Gerry. Two weeks after the fateful date, Mary Jane mentioned in a letter to Bert that Ben might want shift to a "nice, friendly correspondence" since "that's as far as it will go in her case." It's unclear whether Bert delivered the advice, but if he did, it had little effect on his smitten friend. Four days later Mary Jane wrote:

> For a person who met a girl only once, I'd say Ben has it bad or else he has a good ... [indecipherable]. I don't want to shatter his hopes if he has them but he should take things easy. Just a little friendly advice, that's all.

Nine months later, in another letter to Bert, Mary Jane wrote that she was "glad to hear that Ben found a girlfriend for himself. I liked him and think he's such a swell fellow."

Things went well between Bert and Mary Jane on that furlough. On one date they went to an amusement park where he convinced her to go on a roller coaster, something she was deathly afraid of. It spoke eloquently of her total trust in him. He also offered her his wings—the

Bert's wings became a complicated issue in his long-distance romance with Mary Jane. (The Ibelle family)

graceful sterling silver medal awarded to airmen when they completed their flight certification.

Based on her letters, Mary Jane found this offering even more unnerving than the roller coaster, which had scared the daylights out of her.

The day Bert arrived in Florida, he received a long letter from Mary Jane that included her reaction to their week together.

> July 7, 1944
> Dear Bert:
>
> … I received your letter and the way you wrote certain things was really wonderful. You asked me to consider each point and answer them. I'm going to make an attempt but I don't know if I can express myself clearly or not.
>
> You are quite right when you say we have many friends, likes, and dislikes in common. I also believe that we understand each other pretty well and are quite content in each other's company. The last fact is one of the things I have often thought about. I'm content and happy in your company because I have all the confidence in the world in you, as proven by the roller coaster ride. You weren't just kidding when you said I was deathly afraid to go. I went because you asked me to go and because I know you wanted me to try and overcome the frights I have of them. I knew I had you beside me, so I said yes.
>
> As for my actions that last night, I can't begin to explain.… When you offered me your wings, I really wanted to accept them but I didn't think it was quite fair to you. You seemed to see it so differently. I thought that by taking them, you would take me wrong. Maybe I did wrong or maybe I did right. I don't know. To tell the truth, I'm a very confused girl. But believe me, I have done a lot of thinking about the whole thing.
>
> Love, Mary Jane.

CHAPTER 6

Deployed

A few weeks after the furlough, Bert received a letter from Fran, who was preparing to ship overseas.

> July 18, 1944
> Hello you old knobhead:
>
> How's everything with you, the Air Corps, and Mary Jane? I hope you made out okay on the rest of that furlough. If you failed, man, I'm going to give you a few lessons on the fine art of love.... When I got back to Kentucky, my girl was sorry she didn't come to Hartford with me, but I made up for the lost days. No kidding, if she had come home with me, I believe we would have gotten married. When I finally got back, she asked, "Why didn't we get married?" ... Well, no use moaning. There are still plenty of years ahead.

The next communication from Fran was an Army V-mail—a single sheet of paper smaller than a postcard that soldiers and families used to send quick messages. The Army encouraged the use of V-mail because it was faster and more reliable than the postal service. But soldiers generally didn't like them because they were so short. Fran got around that by writing in a tiny script that was so immaculate, he could fit twice as much material on the tiny slips of paper.

August 3, 1944
What say luvah?

Wow, you're really on the stick. I've received a letter and a V-mail from you already and haven't even heard from my gal yet. Anyway, I'm somewhere in the Pacific. Where? Secret; Doing what? Secret, etc. Which is to say that I can't say much except that I'm fine and I wish this damn war were over and we were all raising hell down at the shore with the old gang. Oh yes, just a little more loving and I think you'll get your redhead. Take it easy and keep your flying luck.

Fran.

With a little research, I was able to determine that "somewhere in the Pacific" was Hawaii, where the 96th Infantry Division completed its training before shipping out to the nightmare that awaited them in the Philippines. The Hawaiian assignment explains the jocular tone of his V-mail. The war was still far away, across several thousand miles of ocean.

CHAPTER 7

"We're Not on Vacation Here"

Bert was not impressed with Florida. In a letter to his parents, he said the mosquitoes were "as big as B-29s [the biggest bomber] and come in like 39s [fighter planes]. And now that I've seen it from the air, I can truthfully say that most of Florida is underwater."

The final months of his training were relentless: he was up at 4 a.m. and continued until seven at night. When they trained for night flights, he had to report at 10 a.m. and wouldn't return to the barracks until 2 o'clock the next morning. Bert was so exhausted he brushed his teeth for a week with odd-tasting toothpaste before he realized it was foot powder.

The next letter he wrote to his parents was shocking, given that he was a man who rarely got angry. But apparently Army life had pushed him to his breaking point.

> September 7, 1944
> Dear Folks:
>
> We're now working on a really tough schedule. Today was the easy day. Only 12 hours. Tomorrow and the next day will be 14 hours, the next two days 18 hours, and the last two days 20 hours. I'll have to ask you to not write any more letters giving me hell for not writing. We're not on any vacation here. This is no "having a wonderful time. Wish you were here." We have been learning to go out and kill without being killed ourselves. The guy who gets to go home is going to be the guy who's best prepared. We're learning day and night. Our chances to live must come first, other things come second. We're living under lousy conditions, and we're

> working hours that no civilian would ever stand for. We try to do our best. We can't do any more. We like to get letters but it isn't always possible to drop everything and answer right away. A lot of people get letter after letter, and long ones at that, from guys in the service and therefore everyone is supposed to be able to write. The people don't seem to realize that most of these guys that write these long letters every day are sitting on their dead rectums in some orderly room from 9 a.m. to 5 p.m. and the worst they'll ever have to face is the possibility of a runaway typewriter. The guys here who are working heavy schedules and still writing long letters are giving up their few hours of sleep and sitting in a lice-filled latrine where there are two or three 40-watt bulbs and a million mosquitoes. The rest of us write when we get a little time, and then get hell for it. I know I'm falling down on the job, but please don't remind me of it. It's hard enough as it is.

Wow, he was coming unglued. But it wasn't surprising—sleep deprivation, impending combat, and unrequited love—that's a few too many boulders for any person to carry in their backpack.

After venting his frustration, Bert pulled himself together and continued the letter in a normal manner for several pages.

> September 7, 1944 [continued]
> .... The flying down here is swell. We've been flying all over Florida, up into Georgia and took two flights to Cuba.... We went down to 2000 feet over Cuba and circled several times. I wish we could have landed. Cuba is the nicest country I've ever flown over. Sometime I'm going back there to see it from the ground.
>
> Our bombardier has one of the highest accuracy ratings in the outfit. In fact, one day he put 4 of his bombs right in the center of a cross from 20,000 feet. Our navigator is just as good. On our second Cuban trip he gave his ETA and he only missed by 15 seconds. As for the pilots, I believe that they're the best in the country. The rest of the crew is also swell.
>
> Well, I have to close for now as it's 12 p.m. and I have to get up at 3 a.m. for a morning flight. Good night and sweet dreams.

What he chose not to mention in his letter home was that their original bombardier was a disaster and nearly caused Bert to join the 15,000 American airmen who died in training.

In addition to his main duty as waist gunner, Bert was responsible for arming the bombs as they approached their target. To do this, he had to walk out on a narrow metal catwalk that ran the length of the bomb bay. I call it a catwalk, but it was more like a balance beam. It was 5 inches wide and about 10 feet long. To arm the bombs, he had to crouch down with one foot on the balance beam and the other on a strut below the bombs, then pull the fuses one by one from each bomb. Because the space was so small, he had to perform this duty without a parachute. Although the bomb bay doors were closed—at least in theory—they would open automatically if he were to lose his balance and fall on them. And if a bomb load was inadvertently released, they would take him along for the ride. Here's how Bert explained the incident five decades later:

> Our bombardier was dangerously inept. He opened the bomb bay doors while I was activating the bomb fuses, leaving me on a precarious perch without a parachute and gazing down at ten thousand feet of nothing. He repeated the error on our very next flight. The end came when he mistook the officers' club for his target and nearly dumped a string of practice bombs into that sacrosanct edifice.

During every mission, it was Bert's job to walk out on the bomb bay catwalk as they neared 10,000 feet to remove the fuse pins from the bombs. (The Ibelle family)

Fortunately for everyone involved, they got a new bombardier before they left for the war. Judging from her next letter, Bert must have written to Mary Jane about the incident.

September 5, 1944
Dear Bert:
You fellows sure do have nine lives. You always seem to be in some dangerous position. I suppose it would be silly to say take care of yourself, but even so, I mean it.

★★★

Life on the home front was no picnic either. Mary Jane's letters provide a glimpse of what the war was like for those left behind. There may not have been anyone shooting at them, but for thousands of young women like Mary Jane, the war was stealing their youth. She was 19 years old, less than a year out of high school, and working her first job. This was supposed to be a time of excitement, freedom, and social exploration. You only get one chance at these years, and if you miss them, you don't get a second shot.

When Mary Jane went on lunch break, the streets of the city were filled with women. If she went into a shop or a restaurant—women. When she returned to the office, her co-workers were all women. The only young men in the city were soldiers on furlough looking for a good time. The only other men were those too old to serve. As Mary Jane noted in one letter to Bert, that didn't leave much of a life for women in the prime of their youth: "The only thing I do for entertainment is go to the show [movies] with the girls. There isn't much else to do here. Of course, I could always try picking up the servicemen, but that's not for me."

The absence of young men was even more apparent at the beach in Old Lyme, Connecticut.

August 30, 1944
Dear Bert:
... This place has really changed. All the older girls are with the young fellows who are 16 or 17. Most of these fellows used to go with my [younger] sister's gang but of late they prefer the older girls. And if you don't think this is the talk of the beach, you're

Just the Girls: Lunch break at City Hall (Mary Jane in the middle). (The Ibelle family)

> mistaken. Mary Lynch, who is 24 and a school teacher, has been going out with a fellow who is 17 and just graduated from Weaver High.

Bert must have been making some headway, because during the summer months she seemed to waver a bit.

> July–August 1944
> .... I wish it were in my power to give you an answer to that ever-prevailing question. I could say there isn't anything but friendship as far as I'm concerned, or I could say that you are the one and only. The only trouble is that neither is the truth....
>
> I'm not going to comment on your personal ideas of religion. There are some things you said that I agree with and others that I didn't. You say all we really would need is a little tolerance and you aren't wrong. The question is would our tolerance be lasting. You are so right in many of your ideas, Bert. A true and lasting love has to have faith, confidence, loyalty, and understanding to make

things right. It takes a lot more than just the word "love" to make a happy life. That word is so often misused but you seem to know the real meaning of the word.

Although she was no closer to resolving her romantic logjam, the scales seemed to be evening out between Bert and his rival. In mid-September, a powerful hurricane swept up the East Coast and hammered Old Lyme. Waves toppled portions of the seawall, flooded the first floor of waterfront cottages, and ripped the front porch off a nearby cottage, depositing it a block away. The Pierce cottage was undamaged because it sat on slightly higher ground, but the wind wiped out power for the entire town.

September 15, 1944
Dear Bert:

I am sitting in my room at the cottage with a single candle as my only light. There isn't any electricity since the hurricane came through yesterday.

All the cottages are lit up with candles. If the situation isn't corrected by tomorrow, we will be using a wood stove to cook our meals. I guess I'm just a pioneer girl at heart! ... Gee we sure had some fun during the short time you were home in July. When I reread your letters, I get quite lonesome. I don't know why, but many times when I'm in such a mood, I think of you. You certainly have been swell. All my memories of you and the time we spent are so darn pleasant.

After reading your letters, I got to thinking about your wings. There's nothing I would like better than to wear them but still, I don't feel sure about asking you to send them. Maybe it's because I feel I should wear them under different circumstances. Of course, you said they were mine regardless.

I never thought I was a person who was fickle but maybe I am after all. I thought it was Bill that I really wanted, but now I'm in a fog.

It's not hard to imagine Bert reading that letter over and over while lying in his cot adjacent to the Florida everglades, swatting mosquitoes the size of B-29s. He probably wasn't thrilled by her description of their time together as "so darned pleasant," but when the power went out and she was left in the dark, it was him, Bert Ibelle, that she chose to write to by candlelight. He had visited Mary Jane's cottage on occasion, so he could easily envision the scene: the big stone fireplace, the beadboard walls, the sounds of surf and the smell of seaweed wafting in through the open windows. And most of all, that face glowing in the candlelight as she furrowed her brow and concentrated on the words she was writing … to him!

A few weeks later, Mary Jane wrote a letter accepting Bert's wings. She made it clear that this was neither a declaration of love nor a decision to choose him over Bill Harney. "You said they were mine regardless, but maybe you've changed your mind since."

Bert hadn't changed his mind. So she accepted the wings and wore them proudly. It was about this time that Mary Jane's letters began to take on a more romantic tone.

> October 3, 1944
> …. Old Man Moon is shining beautifully tonight. You are probably seeing it from a plane right now. I certainly do remember that night on the private beach about two years ago. It was during "that" summer. It was simply beautiful that night with the moon at its best, lighting a pathway to heaven and peace….
>
> PS: I don't care how short your letters are as long as I hear from you.

Despite her growing feelings for Bert, she remained paralyzed by her fear that by following her impulses, she would hurt him in the end.

> October 22, 1944
> Dear Bert:
>
> The only way I can talk with you tonight is to write, so that's exactly what I'm going to do. Your picture is sitting up on my dresser smiling at me now, so I feel as though I were really talking with you even though we are separated by many thousands of miles…. Quite some time ago, I made a decision about you and

Bill but I'm not sure I made the right one. I can't make a decision very well now because neither of you are here to help me. The thing that frightens me the most is that I might hurt you in some way. That's the one thing I pray I won't do. I may be a problem to you Bert, but believe me I'm more of a problem to myself. I really can't figure it out....

Loads of love.

Mary Jane

Mary Jane would probably be mortified to see these letters in print. As adults, many of us are a bit horrified by our 19-year-old selves. But if she seems dramatic or self-involved, we should cut her some slack. She was struggling to write about love—and what could be more difficult than that? She was also trying to be honest, direct, and kind all at the same time; and how many of us can perform that juggling act with any measure of grace?

Soon after Bert's furlough, the crew shipped north to Hunter Field in Savannah, Georgia, where they picked up their new B-17 and prepared to fly it to Europe.

November 8, 1944.

Dear Folks:

.... I called Mary Jane Monday night. It sure was good to hear her voice again. She's really a wonderful girl, and someday I hope she'll be part of the family. I imagine you realized that long ago though.

CHAPTER 8

The Boy on the Porch

Sometime during my teenage years, my grandmother told me this story: "When your father was 10 years old, we were sitting on the porch together when Mary Jane walked by. She must have been nine years old at the time. Your father turned to me and said, 'I'm going to marry that red-headed girl someday.'"

True story? Who knows. What I can say for certain is that my grandmother was a no-nonsense woman who did not suffer from the family affliction of embellishing stories. Knowing my father, this story makes complete sense. Bert Ibelle, the man I knew as Dad, was every bit as persistent and singled-minded as that 10-year-old boy on my grandmother's porch.

In case you haven't guessed by now, Mary Jane is my mother. Although this always seemed like destiny to me, I was stunned to stumble upon that box of letters and learn that it was far from certain on that day when my father flew over Hartford on his way to the war. I knew they had dated in high school and assumed they were an item by the time my father joined the Army. I had heard of Bill Harney, but assumed he was just a brief high school flame. I had no idea my father went to war on the losing end of the biggest battle of his life.

What spurred the transition from dearest friend to husband is lost to me forever. What I do know is that they were married for 62 years and did everything together. I heard very few stories about the war, but many about their storybook years at Dartmouth together. My mother worked in the admissions office after they were married, and Hanover remained a paradise on earth for them the way the cottage at Old Lyme Shores was for me. I can attest to how beautifully they complemented each other in the world. My mother was an extrovert—outgoing, sunny, and a bit of a chatterbox. She made friends everywhere they went. My father was more reserved, but he came to life in my mother's presence. In many ways, they were awed by each other.

Oddly, I never heard anyone—including my father—refer to my mother as Red. It's just one more of those little mysteries that will never have an answer.

Like most of us, I'm a combination of my father and mother, so I recognize their virtues and their foibles in myself. Still, there was something spooky about watching my mother inch closer to the precipice of saying "I love you," then get spooked and backpedal to the safety of "confusion." I knew that dance all too well. It took me six years to finally propose to my wife, and the reason was the same: a determination not to hurt someone. I had a deep mistrust of my ability to recognize love when it came. I was not Fran. Love did not hit me like a rocket. I was more like my mother—paralyzed, partly by the fear that I didn't have the capacity to truly love and partly by my inability to recognize it when it arrived in a form other than a rocket. I was stunned to learn that it didn't hit my mother that way either. Fortunately, we both overcame our shared disability and eventually said the words that changed our lives forever.

This wasn't the only trait I inherited from my mother. Whatever modest athletic skills I had, came from the Pierce side of the family. My mother's brother was a national-caliber sprinter and she always told my brother and I that she was the one who taught him how to run. She also claimed to have taught the boys on the high school football team how to drop kick, which was still in vogue back then. "That's great mom," we said, not taking her claims too seriously. I never saw her do anything more athletic than go for a walk.

Then one day when my brother and I were middle-aged and tossing a football in the side yard at the cottage, an errant pass bounced over to where my parents were having a glass of wine. My mother was in her mid-seventies at the time and her knees were shot. She bent down with a groan to pick up the ball, then casually threw it back to me in a perfect spiral—15 yards; right into my hands.

I tossed the ball back to her.

"Do that again," I said.

She threw me another perfect spiral.

Life is full of little surprises.

★★★

My father had a little surprise of his own waiting for me.

I loved my parents and they loved me, but at times I also felt oddly out of place in our family. My parents were creatures of habit. Their routines were pleasant enough, but to me, they were ruts worn so deep, they could never climb out. My parents, of course, had no interest in climbing. They moved happily through the predictable patterns of their lives—work, bridge, golf, poker, cookouts, and summers at the cottage. It was a nice life. But I was a restless kid, and all that pleasantness seemed like Purgatory. Adventure was pretty hard to come by in a suburb of Hartford, a city known as the "Insurance Capital of the Nation." Let's face it, that moniker doesn't make the pulse quicken like "The Big Easy" or "The Mile High City."

But I did my best. As my father napped on the couch with *Oliver Twist* splayed over his face, a buddy and I secretly hitchhiked around southern New England. We'd start early in the morning, stood on opposite sides of the road and stuck out our thumbs. Whichever one got the first ride, that's where we went. When the first driver dropped us off, we'd do the same, hitching on opposite sides of the road and taking the first ride in either direction. Sometimes we'd zigzag aimlessly across northern Connecticut; other times we'd end up in another state. It didn't matter. The point was to be going, and to enjoy the surprising variety of people who were willing pick up two teenagers holding a sign that said "Anywhere." We got rides from hippies smoking marijuana, mothers driving their kids to practice, college professors bound for Amherst or Connecticut College, and migrant farm workers on their way to the tobacco fields along the Connecticut River. One time a rich guy in a Bentley picked us up and displayed an unnerving interest in my left knee. But once I established the rules of non-engagement, even the aristocrat with the roaming hand turned out to be a pretty nice guy.

The challenge was to get home in time for dinner so our parents wouldn't suspect what we were up to. If they ever found out, they'd kill us. We knew they had no sense of adventure and wouldn't understand our urgent need to explore the world. Not our parents.

Then I came across this entry in my father's war diary:

> **November 23, 1944**
> Hitchhiked to Reykjavik today. Walked most of the way in a freezing gale. Got rides from a Dane in a '36 Chrysler and later a young Dane driving a fish truck. Saw how the people lived along the way. Used sign language with two Danes who couldn't speak English. Interesting.

It was a message across seven decades. Dad? Is that you?

CHAPTER 9

"I'm Having the Time of My Life"

Following their nail-biter landing at the head of the Greenland fjord, the crew of "Mr. Bones" spent the next three days waiting for the weather to clear before they flew on to Iceland. In his next letter home, Bert provided what has to be one of the most unusual statements made by a man on his way to war.

> November 21, 1944
> Dear Folks:
> I can't tell you where I am or how I got here. But I can tell you that I'm temporarily somewhere in Iceland. I'm feeling fine and having the time of my life.

The crew of "Mr. Bones" was a random assortment of young men from vastly different backgrounds and most of them were just as green as Bert. There was one exception.

Frank Mullally, the radioman, was nine years older than Bert and had been a commercial artist before the war. He was on his second tour of duty in the Army Air Corps. After he completed 40 missions on B-26s in North Africa, he went home to his advertising job and quickly decided that "civilian life was too chicken." So he signed up for another tour of combat.

Bert quickly recognized that Frank was determined to see as much of the world as possible and that his previous service in North Africa gave him the knowledge he needed to do it. "I stuck close to Frank and experienced a great deal that I otherwise would have missed," he wrote in his retirement-age recollections.

Bert and Frank were a perplexing pair. Bert—the man who produced a war memoir that was factually engaging but devoid of introspection—spent his adult life as a clinical psychologist. He maintained a lifelong passion for the theater, landed the lead roles in his high school plays, and continued to act while at Dartmouth; yet in life, he was loath to explore the subtleties of human emotion.

Frank—the man who signed up for a second tour of combat because civilian life was "too chicken"—became a Franciscan priest after the war and spent the next 50 years as a missionary in Bolivia, walking from village to village bringing comfort and spiritual support to the people of the Andean highlands.

On their second day in Iceland, Frank and Bert decided to see a bit of the arctic island. Rather than take a bus, Frank insisted that they hitchhike because they'd experience more of the country that way. They experienced more than they bargained for.

Frank Mullally was a commercial artist before the war but became a Franciscan priest for the next half century. (The Ibelle family)

As they were leaving the base, they asked a soldier with a thick Scottish accent how far it was to Reykjavik. He told them it was 15 kilometers; or that's what they thought he said. What the Scotsman actually said was that it was 50 kilometers (roughly 30 miles).

It was late November in Iceland, which meant that the sun didn't rise until 10:30 a.m. There was also "a slight gale" blowing in from the North Atlantic. But this was the 20-year-old Bert Ibelle, not the 50-year-old man on the couch with a book splayed over his face. He was with a war veteran nine years his senior, hitchhiking through a foreign land just south of the Arctic Circle. It was going to take a lot more than a November gale to dampen his spirits.

A British lorry gave them a lift to the edge of the air base, then they turned east and started walking. This was not the Iceland of magnificent waterfalls and steaming thermal springs. The airfield was at the tip of Iceland's westernmost peninsula, a land where barren flatlands were covered by knee-high vegetation flattened by the icy winds. They walked for miles through the open country without getting a ride. In one of the villages, they stopped to watch children playing in the schoolyard and Bert displayed his naivete in a letter home when he marveled that the kids were "exactly like any normal American school children at play."

They dallied to watch fishermen drying their nets as their boats tossed about on the cresting waves, then walked to a second village that was mourning the crew of a fishing boat lost at sea. Any romantic notions they had about a fisherman's life evaporated quickly.

> November 21, 1944
> Dear Folks:
> The more I saw of Iceland the more I realized that here was a small nation of some of the most rugged, hard-working people in the world. I soon came to the conclusion that most of us from the States could never exist under the adverse conditions that these people seemed to be so content and happy with.

After walking for nearly two hours, they got their second ride. Bert's attention to the make and year of the car perplexed me until I remembered that he was writing to his father, who was a car salesman.

> November 21, 1944 (continued)
> … We got our second ride from a Dane with a '36 Chrysler (right-hand drive). This was the first time we had encountered the European style of driving on the wrong side of the road. This fellow, however, used all of the road and more. The way he drove over those icy roads was more than amazing. It was almost suicide. Several times we expected to be picking ourselves out of the ditch, but with the Grace of God, and the help of a stray boulder, we would bounce back onto the road like a billiard ball hitting the cushion.

> Somehow, he managed to stay in one piece for the few miles he took us.... When we finally parted ways, he took off slipping and skidding as before, and I was willing to lay down money that without the aid of our sweat and anxiety, we could read his obituary in the morning paper.

Throughout the terrifying ride, the Dane slammed on the brakes, then tromped on the accelerator as he fishtailed around corners, laughing and talking throughout each treacherous maneuver. Looking back on the experience from his retirement, Bert diagnosed the man as hypomanic, and realized that they were fortunate to have survived his unbridled glee.

Once free of the 1936 Deathmobile, Frank and Bert trudged for two more hours into an icy headwind, still believing the 15-kilometer myth. Each time they crested a rise in the countryside, they expected to see the city. But each time there was nothing but more tundra, dotted by an occasional farmhouse. Bert marveled that the landscape did not include a single tree. Unfortunately, the other thing missing from the expansive views were cars, which made hitchhiking a challenge.

Despite its monotony, Bert was entranced by the land's stark beauty. Again, his observations were influenced by the fact that he was writing to his father, who had grown up on a Connecticut farm.

> November 21, 1944 (continued)
> ... We became aware of how vitally important the fishing industry is to the Icelanders. They do just enough dairying to provide for their needs. Neither the soil nor the climate is adaptable to large-scale farming. Vegetation is scarce and trees are non-existent. Their livestock consists almost entirely of goats and Shetland ponies. Cows and horses are few and far between. They can't take the climate.

After walking through a village "with a name as long as its main street," they were picked up by a teenager driving a fish truck. They marveled at the cleanliness of this truck, which solidified their impression of the Icelanders as a noble and orderly breed. They rode to the outskirts of Reykjavik in the back of the truck, fighting frostbite while fantasizing about plunging their frozen hands into the steaming-hot springs that now lined the side of the road. Once in Reykjavik they were again surprised by what they saw.

> November 28, 1944 (continued)
> ... I was expecting to see the Hollywood version of Scandinavia, but Reykjavik was very sleek and modern, and every third or fourth shop was a bookstore. They are a progressive people.

CHAPTER 10

"It Was Exotic in the Extreme"

The smell was overpowering. They were surrounded by the cacophony of street vendors, camels, jugglers, and beggars. They had flown from Iceland to Wales and then on to Morocco, and were now standing in the middle of the Marrakesh market. It was their second and more conventional attempt to see the place.

Bert and Frank's first attempt came soon after landing in the African desert. It involved climbing the fence that surrounded the air base so they could get out and explore the place. But their attempt to go AWOL was foiled when the Senegalese guards, armed with "rifles as long as howitzers," fired warning shots. The volleys of gunfire convinced them that it might be wiser to wait until the next day and take the official Army tour.

In a letter to his parents, Bert described the fabled market as having "the worst conditions of filth and disease imaginable."

> November 28, 1944
>
> ... We could smell the stench for several blocks before we actually got there. There were thousands of natives (Arabs mostly) crowding around the shops, which were nothing more than small lean-tos built in the open square. The people were filthy and diseased. Children often had eyes covered with flies attracted by the ooze from their infections. Decaying garbage was everywhere. The people's togas were as dirty as themselves and in most cases practically rotting off their backs. Everyone had open sores. Most of them had mange,

> jaundice, missing eyes, elephantiasis, undeveloped limbs, and just about everything you could think of. Bubonic plague and typhus was the cause of the place being out of bounds.

A half century later in his retirement-age journal, Bert was a bit embarrassed by this description. He attributed his impressions to the official army briefing they received that emphasized the threat of disease and venereal infection from the local population. But even though the warnings had their desired effect, he could still see the magic of the place. In his letter home he also described a fascinating world where men strode through the crowded market with ornate silver daggers tucked into the belts of their traditional djellabas (Bert called them togas). "It was a world apart from our own," he wrote to his parents.

In retirement, his memory of Marrakesh takes on a more romantic slant. He describes acrobats, snake charmers, dancers, and the Blue Men, "who were so-named because their work with dyes stained their skins in vivid color."

> It was exotic in the extreme. When one managed to overlook the dirt, smell, and evident disease, one then saw something out of the *Arabian Nights*.

As colorful as the Marrakesh experience proved to be, it was not the pinnacle of Bert's African adventure. That occurred a few days and 1,400 miles later in Tunis, where they set up a temporary base among the bombed-out ruins at the edge of the city. The next afternoon, Frank burst into the tent in a state of excitement.

★★★

What follows is one of the handful of war stories my father told during well-lubricated family gatherings. My brother and I always assumed that a key part of the story was an exaggeration produced by the combination of repeated telling, audience laughter, and my father's tendency to gradually embellish a well-received story.

As the story goes, Frank returned to the tent that afternoon giddy with excitement and pulled my father aside to show him the fruit of his scavenger hunt around the base. He had been rummaging through some bombed-out buildings when he discovered a treasure—a small box of official Army passes; all of them blank.

Frank set to work using his artistic skills to forge passes for the two of them. My father was hesitant. You've got to remember that he was a college freshman whose idea of a wild time was a winter sleigh ride with Red in Goodwin Park. In most of my father's war stories, he portrays himself as the naïve rube, as he does in this scene, which he recreated in his memoir:

> "Let's go to Tunis," says Frank.
>
> "I don't know. At this point, I'd rather not get in trouble."
>
> "Bert, sit down and think."
>
> I sat.
>
> "Where are you?"
>
> "Tunis."
>
> "Where are you going?"
>
> "Italy."
>
> "And what are you going to do when you get to Italy?"
>
> "Fly combat."
>
> "How long do you think they'll keep you in the guardhouse if they catch you with a phony pass?"
>
> I thought for a moment.
>
> "Let's go."

A bit corny, but this wasn't the part of the story my brother and I doubted. It was the signature on those passes that made us roll our eyes every time my father told the story. So imagine my surprise when I turned the page of his war memoir and, there it was: a photocopy of the forged Army pass, signed—just as my father claimed—by "Major Mistake."

It was true, which meant that my father's other absurd story was also probably true—the one about how he avoided kitchen duty by telling the MP (Military Police) a fake name: George Bernard Shaw.

★★★

The next morning, Frank and Bert used the Major Mistake passes to walk off the base with impunity and hop on a streetcar into Tunis and then a second streetcar to Carthage, where they hired a local boy to give them a tour of the ancient ruins. He described the day in a letter to his parents.

> November 1944
> … I was amazed at how much the children knew. They have no education whatsoever. The young lad we picked up to guide us was about 15 years old. He was teaching his younger brother the business. Both could speak good English, French, Arabic, German, Spanish, and Italian. Find an American of any age who can do that!

Their teenage guide took them to the colosseum, where they visited the prisoner cages and lions' dens, and then took them to the amphitheater. The boy provided details about Roman history and architecture along the way. Bert marveled at the intricate mosaics of the church floors and described how cities of various conquering civilizations were visibly built on top of one another.

The next day, Frank forged two more passes, but when they got to the gate this time, the MP examined the passes line by line. Bert was sure they were about to be thrown in the stockade. He exhaled in relief when the MP finally waved them through, but before they took a half dozen steps, the MP yelled, "Wait!" Bert was sure they were busted:

> With a sinking feeling, I turned to see that the MP was talking to someone in a staff car. I heard him say, "Colonel, these fellows are going into town. Do you mind giving them a ride?" So Frank and I rode to Tunis in style, compliments of Major Mistake.

This time they decided to explore Tunis itself. Frank knew enough French from his previous tour of duty in North Africa to strike up a halting conversation with a pair of guards outside one of the historic palaces. Bert watched as one of the guards went inside, then returned with a black-robed official, who asked, in perfect English, whether the two airmen would like a tour of the palace, which was a residence of the Bey of Tunis.

> November 1944 (continued)
> … The floors were mosaic, the walls were hand-carved and looked like lace, and some rooms had pure gold ceilings. The throne room

> was small and rather disappointing, and the Old Boy's bed looked as uncomfortable as Hell. We went up on the roof and got a wonderful view of the old city. There was a mosque only a few hundred feet away and we were just in time to witness the noon call to prayer. It was quite a sight.

Soon after they left the palace, they came upon one of the historic gates into the Medina (which Frank refers to as the Cas Bas). This is the ancient Muslim section of the city, which was strictly off-limits to servicemen. It was a walled labyrinth of twisting alleys and exotic shops, and naturally they wanted to take a peek. At the tunnel-like gate, Frank struck up a conversation with the Tunisian guard, who gave him "a conspiratorial nod" and turned his back briefly as the two airmen slipped through the archway into the forbidden city.

Their plan had been to take a quick look around and maybe buy something at one of the shops, then return quickly through the gate before they got caught. But as they examined some goods outside a shop, an Arab boy ran up down the narrow street shouting "MPs, MPs." The Jeep went by quickly, but one of the MPs spotted the two AWOL airmen as he passed. Fortunately, the street was too narrow and crowded for the Jeep to turn around, so the MPs had to go out through the gate to turn. Frank and Bert were about to run when a flurry of bedsheets fell over them from the windows above. For a moment, Bert was terrified, but then realized that the Muslim residents were trying to hide them from the police. They pressed up against the wall with the laundry covering them as the returning Jeep sped past. Frank waved a quick thank-you to the women above and then took off down a narrow alley with Bert close behind. After making several quick turns down a series of adjoining alleys, they ducked into one of the shops. Several minutes passed with no sign of the MPs, so they emerged into the street, only to realize they were hopelessly lost. Bert describes their reaction in his war memoir:

> We didn't care. We were enthralled by the sounds, smells, and colors of the native quarter. I remember passing a butcher shop and wondering about the coal-black side of meat that was hung there. As I reached out to touch it, a million flies took wing.

A narrow escape from the military police while AWOL in the Tunis Cas Bas. (Frank Mullally, all drawings are by Mullally, radioman on "Mr. Bones")

They spent an hour wandering the labyrinth of twisting lanes hoping to find one of the five gates that led out of the walled city. Eventually, they came upon some trolly tracks and followed them until they reached a gate just before dusk. Giddy with the high crime they had just pulled off, they caught a bus back to the base.

***

All of this produced a spell of vertigo for me. The man on the couch—the man who followed every rule—had gone AWOL on a forged pass signed Major Mistake so he could explore the forbidden Cas Bas of Tunis. He hitchhiked across Iceland and wrote home about being picked up by a hypomanic Dane who skidded across the icy roads as if rolling your car in the windswept tundra was the national sport.

Maybe we weren't as different as I had always assumed. But if that was true, what happened to my father's sense of adventure? And more important, had my own sense of adventure slipped silently away without my notice? Have I become the man on the couch? It's true that I read a lot. And I do it on the couch. It's also true that I enjoy drifting off to sleep with a book splayed over my face as the winter sun angles in on me through the windows. Is that the image my children have of me?

Thankfully, I was able to talk myself down from that ledge. Yes, I do read a lot; sometimes through closed eyelids. And yes, my house is in danger of collapsing from the weight of all the books. But I also battle storms in my sailboat, hike mountains on several continents, and my wife and I even camped on the ridge of an active volcano so we could witness nature's primordial performance at night.

So I have not become my father, and knowing this allows me to be proud of the many positive traits he bequeathed to me: integrity, kindness, intelligence, loyalty, and diligence. Like my father, I married a woman who I love dearly and is my closest companion. That's not a bad inheritance.

But if my father once burned with the same flame that burns in me, what happened to his thirst for adventure? Maybe the answer lay in the months ahead, for Bert's month-long international romp was drawing to a close—and his war was about to begin.

CHAPTER II

"And My Mother Was Worried About the Germans"

Mud, rain, sleet, snow, and more mud.

This was the Italy that greeted Bert when he finally arrived at the war. Their journey in "Mr. Bones" from the US to Gioia, Italy, took 322 hours, slightly more than 13 days—and the first thing that happened when they landed in Italy is that they lost their plane. It wasn't shot down and it wasn't stollen by joyriding youths—but within hours of landing in Gioia, the Army Air Corps repossessed "Mr. Bones" and shipped it off to places unknown to be flown by other crews. (There is no record of a plane by that name flying missions over Europe, so presumably, the plane was renamed by its new crew.)

Stranded without a plane in a city near the heel of the Italian boot, the crew made the final 170-mile trek to their new home by truck, bouncing along the sloppy, pot-holed roads of southern Italy.

> The rain fell all day, making the movement by truck convoy a rather miserable experience. Passing through some towns, we were cheered—a nice experience. Passing through at least one town, we were stoned—not a nice experience.

Cheers and rocks—it was an eloquent expression of the deep divide among the Italian people over the collapse of the Mussolini government and the advance of the "liberating" Allied forces.

Bert's new home for the duration of the European war was the Sterparone air base, a makeshift landing strip and tent city on a forlorn tract of farmland about a dozen miles inland from the Adriatic coast and 10 miles north of Foggia. They arrived in the middle of the night. It was cold and, of course, raining. The mud was six inches deep with two inches of water on top and they had to set up their tent in the dark.

> Upon arrival, we were unceremoniously dumped, bag and baggage, in front of the supply tent. The supply officer gave us a tent, pegs, and six canvas cots, then told us to set up at the end of one of the company streets. We worked in the rain by flashlight and eventually managed to get things well enough organized so that we could crawl into our cold and soggy beds. When we awoke in the morning, some of the cots had sunk to the level where the legs crossed. Our baggage was afloat. Frank's experience and leadership got us moving—fast.

The first order of business was to dig drainage ditches around the tent to redirect the runoff in hopes of drying the place out a bit. The second priority was the stove, which, judging from Bert's reflections, consumed as much of the crew's attention during the war as enemy antiaircraft guns. He went into great detail about the creation of their stove and took great pride in the ingenuity needed to fashion it out of scrap materials.

They scavenged the airfield for oil drums, cowl flap valves, oil lines, fuse cans—anything they could use to construct their improvised heating stove. They dug a hole in front of the tent pole large enough to hold a 55-gallon drum and filled it with stones that would hold the heat from

Home sweet home: Tents at the Sterparone airfield. (Frank Mullally)

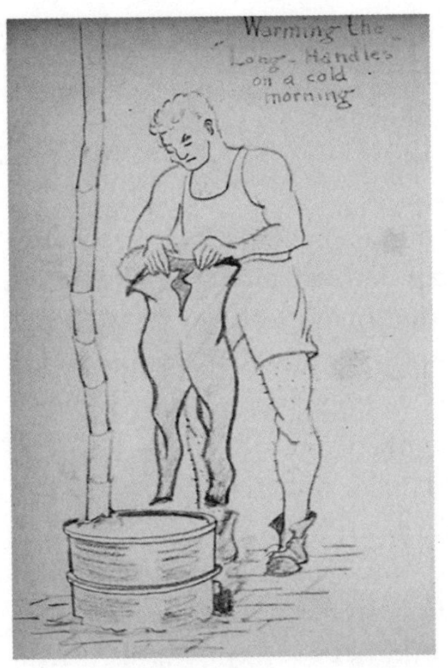

The crew built their crude stove out of scavenged parts from wrecked airplanes and powered it with aviation fuel. It was an object of deep affection because it helped them battle the brutal Italian winter of 1944/45, as well as serving a multitude of additional duties. (Frank Mullally)

the Army-issued gasoline stove they placed on top. Next, they built a chimney out of four-inch-wide fuse cans, which would carry fumes through the roof and, as the pipe heated up, distribute more heat into the tent along the way. The aviation fuel that powered this contraption was stored in a 55-gallon drum positioned just outside of the door of the tent and connected to the stove through scavenged oil lines. They used discarded flap valves to control the drip of fuel into the stove's firebox.

To start a fire, they ran raw gasoline into the stove, lit the fuel with a toilet paper fuse, and as soon as the stove was red hot and the initial fire died down, they began the fuel drip into the firebox, which was vaporized from the heated stones, then ignited and burned with a steady, extremely hot flame.

This display of American ingenuity might strike you as a tad dangerous, given that this all took place inside a canvas tent. The danger was not lost on those who lived in those tents.

> Each stove had its own rhythm and if that rhythm was interrupted, all occupants of that tent dove outside. My mother, god bless her, was worried about the Germans.

★★★

The details about the stove might strike you as a bit dull. They certainly struck me that way the first time I read my father's reflections. There I was, expecting to find a window into the old man's soul, and what I got was a four-page description about how to build a stove out of discarded soup cans.

Was that it? Was this the information he wanted to impart to the world after surviving the most important war in modern history? Is this what he wanted to reflect on after seeing friends shot out of the sky; after his squadron inadvertently bombed some of the most beautiful cities on the planet; after accidentally killing civilians in order to defeat the most powerful and vicious evil the world has ever known? Is it true that the information he most wanted to pass on to posterity—and his children—was how they built their stove?

I was flabbergasted. But on further reflection, I was also pretty confident that I missed the point. This was a group of young men who had been thrown together at random and dropped off in a cold, muddy field in a foreign country on a dark December night. Soon they would have to fight a war, but first there was a more immediate emergency. They were drenched and it was really cold. More than anything else in the world, they wanted to get warm. They could worry about the Germans later.

But there is a deeper significance to their ability to improvise that stove. For this group of boys—and that's what they were—survival was going to depend on their ability to work as a team under enormous pressure. Building that stove was a practice run for the type of cooperation and innovation they would need to survive when things didn't go according to plan over Germany. Working as a team was a skill that would save their lives.

The problem was that my father didn't say any of that. He just described how they built the stove.

Several entries later he was still at it, describing how they built a brick floor for the tent to seal out the dampness and cold. Then, finally, after a dozen pages, a class on emergency radio techniques jogged a paragraph of explanation:

> The class was nothing new for our crew. Ever since we had gotten together, we had been functioning as a team, which we felt involved with every crew member having an intimate knowledge of every other crew member's job. At night, after lights out, Frank would tap messages in code for the rest of us to try to read. Lou was often on the flight line working with the mechanics. He frequently brought the rest of us along so that we would have firsthand knowledge of the workings of our engines. I held informal classes stripping machine guns and had the crew so proficient that while on a night flight and wearing silk gloves they could strip and reassemble their weapons without being able to see the parts. In short, we made every effort to ensure that each of us could do the other guy's job in a pinch. Even more important, we knew not only what we were supposed to do in a crisis, but had absolute confidence in what our fellow crew members would do. This was insurance for survival.

Hemingway's iceberg again. All that detail about how they built their stove was really describing the importance of teamwork, trust, and group ingenuity in the face of unexpected challenges. These were the qualities that would keep them alive.

★★★

The Sterparone airfield was a single 6,000-foot asphalt runway which was laid down in a sea of featureless farmland in the flatlands of eastern Italy. This was not the Italy of travel magazines. It was a flat, rural landscape scattered with crumbling towns that were impoverished before the war and now were even worse.

> January 14, 1945
> Dear Folks:
> … All of the towns are very much the same. They are dirty, messed-up affairs. The main boulevards are wide streets but as you go further off the main drag, the streets become narrower and more crooked. Usually, they're ankle-deep in mud and everyone throws their garbage out into these little alleyways. A good many of them are only six or seven feet wide.… The principal means of transportation is by foot or wagon. These people sure have got

some nice horses and mules. The richest people drive a team of three abreast in front of their carriage. Most of them have two and some of them only have one. Of course, the poorest class walks. The boys that haul wine have a cart just big enough to hold three barrels. The driver sits on the barrel and smokes a clay pipe with a long stem and small bowl. Almost all of the houses are without heat. Everywhere you go you see someone out on the doorstep fanning a large brass pot full of glowing embers. When most of the smoke is gone, they carry the pot inside, and sit around the embers. What a way to live!

PS: Uncle Ben will be interested to know that Frank and I are trying to wade through *The Republic of Plato* by S. A. Richards. It sure is deep and dry, but there's a lot of sense in it.

It's evident from the tone of this letter that the constant rain, mud, and cold had dampened Bert's sense of adventure. He saw nothing exotic

The long walk into town. (The Ibelle family)

about the grinding poverty of southern Italy in 1945. In fact, Italy had done what the Arctic winds of Iceland could not—crush his spirits. He had finally arrived at the war and discovered that his new home was a soggy cot with its legs sunk a foot deep in the mud.

December 7, 1944
Rain. Raided a cracked-up plane and got new valves. Collected wood and materials. Made washbasins out of ammunition cans.

December 9, 1944
Rain. Picked up materials from bomb dump. Built doorway for tent. Much warmer and homier.

December 10, 1944
Rain. Rained like the devil today. Had two inches of water and four inches of mud in the tent. Went to class on escape and evasion all afternoon. Miserable as hell.

December 11, 1944
Rain. Wired up electric lights (swiped the wire). Put valve #5 on stove. Improved heating.

December 12, 1944
Rain. Got bricks for floor and extended one side of tent. Very warm and comfortable in tent tonight.

You get the idea. In his retirement recollections, Bert explained his reference in the first of those entries to "Collected wood and materials":

> Curiously the wood was said to be a mess hall table that disappeared during the night. By some mysterious process, it ended up in our possession and, shortly after dawn it became the framework for our extended tent. Later in the day, we were assigned to look for the missing table, which unfortunately was never found.

It's hard to tell which was the more formidable enemy during those first three weeks in Italy: mud or boredom. It certainly wasn't combat, because there wasn't any. The steady cycle of rain, sleet, and snow grounded the bombers day after day, week after week. They attended briefings, prepared their plane, and went to bed worrying how they would handle themselves in combat—only to have the mission canceled in the morning.

One might think this was a welcomed reprieve. But they were packed six men to a tent with nothing to do. The inactivity only intensified the tension about what was to come. They knew they had to complete a minimum of 35 missions to qualify for discharge, and if they had to fly into the German flak nearly three dozen times to get home, they wanted to get started. Waiting was torture.

The minimum number of missions is a confusing topic. When the United States first entered the war, there was no rule at all. Airmen just fought until they either died or the war ended. With the average lifespan for bomber crews being just 11 missions at this point in the war, this "fly until the end of the war" policy was a virtual death sentence. This took a toll on both the morale and the mental health of bomber crews, a fact that was beginning to reduce their effectiveness in battle. When Air Corps leadership realized this, they instituted 25-mission rule for discharge. However, it soon became clear that airmen were now eligible for discharge too soon to maintain maximum fighting numbers. So the Fifteenth Air Force in Italy created a new, more complicated, rule. It required a minimum number of flights to target, now known as "sorties." If a sortie was long enough or dangerous enough, it could count as two "missions." The new minimum requirement for discharge was 35 sorties or 50 missions. Because most of Bert's missions were both long and dangerous, almost all of them counted as two missions.

Weeks passed and the weather was relentless, so Bert's crew waited nervously for their first combat.

★★★

While they worried about the coming mission, they had one major source of comfort: their plane. The B-17, commonly known as the "Flying Fortress," could carry 6,000 pounds of bombs and was defended by thirteen .50-caliber machine guns that were pointed in every direction—above and below, right and left, front and back. Luftwaffe pilots described attacking a B-17 squadron flying in formation as going after a flying porcupine.

With its long wings and narrow fuselage, the B-17 was a remarkably graceful airplane, despite its heavy armaments.

Those broad, 104-foot wings were also responsible for the legendary durability of the Flying Fortress, which was a good thing, given the fact that Bert's plane got hit on virtually every mission. Most airmen witnessed at least one B-17 that had flown hundreds of miles back to base with two of its four engines out, or its tail shredded by shrapnel, or its fuselage punctured with dozens of holes—or all three.

In spite of its lumbering takeoff, once in flight, "The Big Bird" took on the elegance of a soaring bird of prey.

The tradeoff for this combination of grace, firepower, and durability was an interior that was cramped in the extreme. The main fuselage where Bert served as waist gunner had a diameter of about 7 feet. With the floorboards in, it was barely large enough for a grown man to stand straight. It was so narrow that the gunners in early models bumped into each other constantly while shooting from opposite sides of the plane. Later models solved this problem by staggering the position of the windows on either side of the fuselage so each man could move behind their gun unencumbered.

Despite its heavy armaments, the B-17 was a remarkably graceful airplane. Its endurance was legendary and nearly every squadron had stories of a heavily damaged plane limping home safely against all odds. (The Ibelle family)

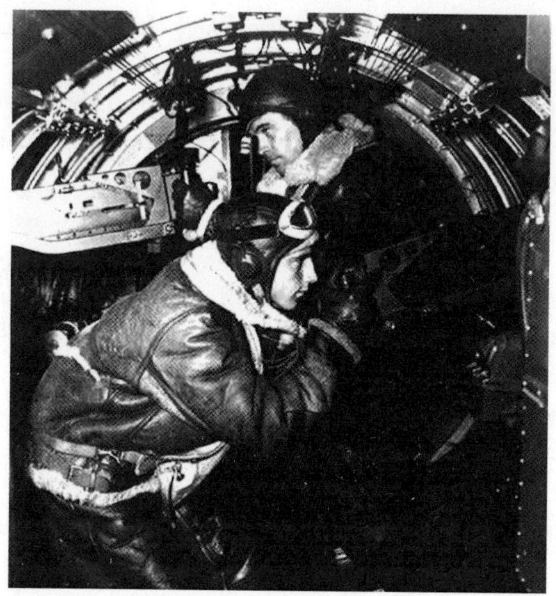

B-17 waist gunners had a tight squeeze during missions that often lasted up to 10 hours. (US Air Force, US National Archives)

In quarters that must have felt like an airborne submarine, they flew 8–10-hour missions, most of that time at the height of Mount Everest with the temperature hovering around 50 degrees below zero. During these missions, that 7-foot aluminum tube was their entire world—and possibly their coffin.

★★★

On Christmas Eve 1944, their mission was canceled yet again. That night, Bert was assigned to guard duty, which meant he'd be up until 4 a.m. He was scheduled for a mission the next day and notes that being assigned guard duty the night before a mission "made for some uncomfortable winter nights and short tempers."

But as he patrolled the planes alone on that freezing December night, he wasn't worried, because everyone knew they didn't fight wars on Christmas Day. During World War I the two armies called a temporary truce on Christmas Eve while German and American troops crawled on their bellies out into No-Man's-Land to decorate a Christmas tree. After they crawled back to their respective trenches, they sang Christmas carols to one another across No-Man's-Land. So Bert was certain he'd have plenty of time to sleep the next morning.

He was in for a surprise.

CHAPTER 12

Into the Inferno

December 25, 1944

Mission to Brux, Germany, oil refinery. 1,300 miles. 8½ hours. 5,000 lbs. of bombs. Ship in element bombed a small town. 6 minutes of intense and accurate flak. Several ships in squadron hit. One to Foggia with badly wounded. Lost one over target—spin. Saw one on fire. Several severely damaged. Third group hit by fighters. Altitude 29,000 feet. −50 degrees. 7½ hours on oxygen.

Christmas Day 1944; Bert's first mission. The target was an oil refinery 50 miles northwest of Prague.

Brux was located in the Sudetenland area of Czechoslovakia that Chamberlain had given to Hitler in order to purchase "Peace In Our Time." Chamberlain's government had described Czechoslovakia as an insignificant little country too distant to be of any consequence. On Christmas Day 1944, it was close enough for us to make contact with it and leave a number of American airmen there—some permanently.

Bert was flying in his usual position as the right waist gunner, which meant he was in the middle of the plane operating a machine gun to shoot down enemy fighter planes. As they passed over Yugoslavia, the other waist gunner, Gene Wisby, pointed out flak in the distance.

The tiny flecks, which looked like grains of pepper, gave me great confidence. "Piece of cake," I thought. My feeling seemed to receive confirmation over Austria when we again viewed this inconsequential stuff in the distance.

The distant flak looked like tiny peppercorns. "Piece of cake," thought Bert—until he got closer. (US Air Force)

Bert's first impression of flak couldn't have been further from reality. Flak was one of the two primary threats to Allied bombers. The other was the fearsome Luftwaffe fighter planes that swooped in on the lumbering bomber formations like angry bees, firing 30 mm cannons with explosive shells that could send a bomber into a flaming spin.

Flak (from the German word *Flugabwehrkanone*) referred to the exploding shells fired by antiaircraft cannons on the ground. The shells were timed to go off at a designated altitude, and when they exploded they sent a shotgun blast of twisted iron shrapnel through the air that could pierce a bomber's fuselage, kill crew members, and cause fuel tanks to explode. As the bombers approached their target, the German antiaircraft guns began firing in rapid succession filling the sky at the bomber's altitude with black explosions as these aerial hand grenades sprayed the sky with flying metal fragments.

Since this was a major threat to Bert's future on this earth, he provided a detailed description of the two primary kinds of flak attacks. The first, and most effective, was tracking flak, which functioned much like skeet shooting: The Germans estimated the speed and altitude of the planes, calculated the time it would take the flak to reach their adversaries, then led the bombers so the flak arrived at the same spot at the same time as the planes. In this type of flak, the guns fired in succession, continually leading the planes to creating a linear series of flak bursts that continued to explode around the planes for quite some time.

In the other option, a barrage flak, every gun was aimed at the same imaginary box that lay in the path of the planes. As the planes approached the box, the guns opened fire so that, seconds later when the bombers entered the imaginary box, the entire area exploded with the thunder of concentrated flak. Tracking flak was a sustained attack while barrage flak was a sudden, but relatively short, flurry of all the firepower Germany had to offer.

> The flak usually began in earnest as the squadron approached the target.
>
> I dutifully hooked on my parachute and donned my flak suit and helmet. I leaned against my window to watch the sight. Suddenly, the whole sky turned black, and just as it did so, our formation turned directly into the inferno. They're crazy, I thought. The six-minute eternity eventually passed and most of us came out the other side. It was the only time I experienced a flak barrage rather than the tracking flak. I later learned that although the barrage is more frightening, it is less deadly than the tracking kind.

Flak barrage: On several missions, flak blew holes through the fuselage around Bert's waist gunner position. "There were only two missions when our plane didn't get shot up pretty bad," he told me. (Frank Mullally)

Bert's Christmas Day introduction to mechanized warfare lasted for eight and a half hours, much of it at minus 50 degrees Fahrenheit in a stratospheric world with little oxygen. About four hours into the mission, the sky exploded with a cascade of thunderous explosions. Flying shards of metal filled the air and smoke from the explosions turned the sky around their plane black.

The Germans had surrounded the oil refinery on three sides with a prisoner-of-war camp, which made it essential that they bomb with extreme accuracy. US heavy bombers took great pride in their Daylight Precision Bombing, which combined use of the innovative Norden bombsight with high-risk mission protocols. For example, the Fifteenth Airforce policy was to engage in no evasive action during the final bomb run, which increased accuracy but made the bombers more vulnerable to enemy flak and fighter attacks.

In his retirement-era recollections, Bert rightfully expressed pride in their precision bombing. But he made no mention of the sentence fragment in his war diary that says that one plane missed the target completely and flattened a nearby village. There are other references in his telegraph-style war journal to burning cities and occasional off-target bomb releases. But in his retirement-age reflections, he never elaborates on this. So we will never know what he thought about inflicting enormous human carnage in order to prevent even greater human carnage—or whether he thought about it at all.

The one time I interviewed him on the subject, he gave the distinct impression that those kinds of moral dilemmas were not something he concerned himself with. He had a job to do, and he did it. Knowing my father as the smart, caring, educated man that he was, it's hard for me to fathom that moral stance. But maybe that's what a person has to do in order to live with the things they are forced to do during a war. How on earth would I know? The most dangerous fight I ever got into was with a storm at sea, and that's a battle without morality.

★★★

During that first Christmas Day raid, Bert watched several of the bombers around him go down in flames. In all, he said the Germans shot down 14 bombers that day. Those who made it back to the base were treated to a traditional holiday turkey. Bert wrote home that night and did everything he could to convince his parents that he was safe:

> December 25, 1944
> Dear Folks:
> Merry Christmas! Last night I received the finest Christmas present a fellow could ask for: the first mail from you, Red, Aunt June, Uncle Ben and Aunt Hazel. Man! What a boost to the spirits that was!!!... We've started our missions, so we're on the road home. Don't worry, we haven't encountered any fighters yet and although the flak is intense, it doesn't last long. We have the best training and the best equipment. Everything is in our favor. We get plenty scared at times, which is only natural, but if you start to worry (which I hope you won't) remember this: From what I've seen, it amazes me how they can throw so much and hit so little. We learned to pray as we never have before. The danger is short and the odds are all in our favor. Don't Worry!
> PS: The scenery in Austria, Yugoslavia and Germany is pretty swell. The Alps are some hills.

Despite his brave talk, Bert was well-aware of the Russian roulette he was playing with every mission. With one bullet in the six chambers, the odds of surviving a single round of Russian roulette are 83 percent. As odds go, that's not bad. But with stakes that serious, just about any of us would be piss-in-our-pants terrified to spin the barrel and pull the trigger. Yet that's exactly what Bert did every time the wheels of his B-17 left the ground.

I have not been able to find any reliable statistics about the survival rate for B-17 airmen during the final year of the war. Several sources cite a 70 percent survival rate for the war in general. That's considerably worse than Russian roulette. But this statistic is, if accurate, also deceiving because the survival rate varied greatly depending on the period of the war. The worst period was in 1943 when the Luftwaffe was at its most dominant and the Allied forces did not have fighter planes with the range needed to accompany bombers all the way to the target. As a result, the B-17s of 1943 were sitting ducks during the most dangerous part of the mission. In early 1943, the average life expectancy for a B-17 crewman was 11 missions and several unattributed sources say the odds of survival were somewhere around 50 percent. If that's accurate, it means that B-17 crews were playing Russian roulette with three bullets in the chamber.

But the odds were much better than this by the final year of the war. By the second half of 1944, the Allies had substantially weakened the Luftwaffe and added long-distance protection for the bombers with the new P-51 fighter escorts. As a result, the odds of survival improved dramatically. There's no solid statistic for 1945 when Bert flew most of his missions, but it's safe to say that B-17 bomber crews were now flying with just one bullet in the Russian roulette chamber. Much better—but still, no thanks.

And Bert knew that he had to spin that barrel and pull the trigger 35 times before he could go home.

★★★

It's worth noting that once he arrived in Italy, the content of Bert's letters was severely limited by Army censors. Anything that would undermine morale back home was forbidden. Soldiers knew they were not allowed to write about fear, doubt, depression, despair, anger, guilt, or anything else that might undermine the image of the soldier as a stoic hero willing to brave physical hardship and mortal danger for the good of America and mankind.

Because of the heavy restrictions, his letters home were fairly short and focused on mundane details like how much money he was sending home and requests for underwear, cookies, and film. Another recurring theme was his assurances that everything was going smoothly and there was no cause for worry. In his zeal to convince his parents that he was in no great danger, he described a world of snowball fights, impromptu baseball games, and the mundane activities of daily life. For example, several months later, one of his letters included the following passage:

> March 8, 1945
> Right now, Casey is writing, Lou's sleeping, Gene and Frank are playing chess, and Ben's washing clothes in an old slop bucket. Very exciting, eh!

There were also limitations based on what might give the enemy hints about troop movements, fighting power, or strategy. Soldiers weren't even supposed to tell their loved ones where they were. So before he left, Bert established a code to let his parents know what part of the world he was in. The code was based on the ancestry of his high school friends. If he was in England, he would write that he ran into Bruce, if in Italy he'd say he ran into Fran, and if he was in the Pacific, he would say he ran into Kenney.

As his letters indicate, this code proved unnecessary since Bert was able to tell them straight out that he was somewhere in Italy. But the Army censors remained quite active, cutting pieces of information that were far from secret, as my father pointed out in his retirement:

> The secrecy about where we were and what we were doing was a bit ludicrous. When we arrived at Sterparone, Axis Sally greeted us on her nightly radio broadcast: "Welcome to Ted Frink [his pilot] and his crew who have just joined the 483rd Bomb Group." All crews got a similar welcome. Also, I don't remember more than one or two occasions on which Axis Sally didn't announce our primary target for the next day and our time of arrival. Her sign-off was always a cheery, "We'll be waiting for you!" It seemed that the only thing she didn't know was our assigned altitude.

Axis Sally! She was the sexy voice of treason; an American working for the Nazis who used her radio broadcasts from Berlin to undermine the morale of American soldiers. Her goal was to plant seeds of doubt, by convincing them that their corrupt president had sent them to slaughter and that he was using them as sacrificial lambs for the British and the Jews. Her show, *Home Sweet Home* began with a train whistle, an evocative sound designed to make soldiers homesick. One of the running themes of her broadcasts was the infidelity of girlfriends and wives back home, "especially if you boys get all mutilated and do not return in one piece."

So why did GIs listen? The answer was simple: the music. Axis Sally played the hottest swing and big band hits of the era. The propaganda was deftly slipped in between the songs. Most soldiers insisted that they listened only for the music or to laugh at the propaganda. It's impossible to say whether the bomber crews of the 483rd viewed Sally as a seductress or a joke, but either way, she was very much on their minds.

Imagine yourself in Bert's tent during those first nights in Italy: You're lying on your cot with its legs sunk eight inches into the mud. Outside that thin canvas wall, miles of hauntingly bleak countryside stretches to the horizon in every direction. You're listening to Benny Goodman on the radio to get your mind off the next day's mission and just as the song ends, the sexy voice of Axis Sally breaks in to welcome your pilot by name—"Ted Frink and his entire crew"—to Italy. How on earth did she know your names and that you had just arrived? Later, when your missions finally begin, this same woman announces the target of your mission and signs off by saying, "We'll be waiting for you, boys."

Mildred Gillars, aka Axis Sally, was raised in Ohio and enrolled at Ohio Wesleyan University as a drama major. She left before graduation to seek fame in Greenwich Village, where she spent her twenties working a series of odd jobs while taking acting lessons and landing a few bit parts in Vaudeville.

But fame never came. Not even modest success. So in 1929, she moved to Paris for two years, then followed a boyfriend to Algiers, where she worked as a dressmaker's assistant until the relationship ended. After the breakup, she bounced around Europe for a few years before settling in Dresden, Germany, where she studied music and taught languages.

Her big break came in 1940 when she landed a job as an announcer for German State Radio. When the American government advised all US citizens to leave Germany in 1941, Gillars chose to stay because her fiancé at the time, a German physicist, refused to marry her if she moved back to America. Even though she stayed, the marriage never took place because her fiancé was killed on the Eastern Front.

Gillars continued her work as a radio announcer and voice actress in radio plays. Then in 1942, Joseph Goebbels, the German minister of propaganda, decided that he needed someone with an American accent to persuade Americans to oppose the war. Gillars fit the bill.

Using the stage name "Midge at the Mike," Gillars portrayed herself as a playful vixen who was worried that the boys were headed for slaughter in a pointless war. Many GIs would have been surprised to learn that Axis Sally was 44 years old. But this was the age of radio; a time when celebrities were just a voice and it was up to the audience to fill in the rest.

Mildred Gillars, aka Axis Sally. (Alamy, Everett Collection Historical)

GIs gave "Midge" a variety of nicknames, including "The Bitch of Berlin" and "The Berlin Babe." Then, during a radio interview, she described herself saying, "I'm the Irish type—a real Sally." The name stuck and she became universally known as Axis Sally.

By 1943, there were actually two Axis Sallys—one operating out of Berlin and another broadcasting from Rome. GIs in Italy received both broadcasts. The Italian Sally, Rita Zucca, was also an American. She was born in 1912 in New York City, where her father owned a successful restaurant in midtown Manhattan named Zucca's Italian Garden. As a teenager, she attended a convent school in Florence, then returned to New York to work in the family business. In 1938, she moved back to Italy because the Mussolini government was about to repossess the family land because it was owned by foreigners. To avoid this, Zucca established Italian citizenship and renounced her status as a US citizen.

Zucca was working a mundane job as a government typist in 1943 when Mussolini decided he needed his own Axis Sally. Zucca won the job and quickly became known for her sexy voice and cooing sendoff, "A sweet kiss from Sally."

Both Sallys were eventually apprehended, but their fates were quite different. Zucca was arrested in Turin shortly after the German surrender, but could not be prosecuted in American courts because she had renounced her US citizenship eight years earlier. She was eventually tried in an Italian court, served a mere nine months in prison, and lived as a free woman in Italy until her death in 1998 at age 86.

Rita Zucca, the Italian Axis Sally. (Rita Zucca Helge Collection N.325)

As an American citizen, Gillars did not fare so well. Following the German surrender, she disappeared for nearly a year, living under an assumed name while the Allies struggled to track her down. When she was finally captured, she became the first woman in American history to be tried for treason. In January 1949, she was convicted and sentenced to 30 years in prison. She served 12 years, and upon her release in 1961, she moved back to Columbus, Ohio, where she taught language and music at Our Lady of Bethlehem Convent. She died of colon cancer in 1988 at the age of 87.

★★★

With one mission under his belt, Bert felt like he was finally contributing to the war effort. He was also relieved to find that he handled himself well in battle and "wouldn't let down my crewmates or myself."

At 3 a.m. on December 28, 1944 the crew was rousted from their cots for their second mission. This time their goal was to drop 6,000 pounds of bombs over Regensburg, Germany. Bert described the mission as a "milk run," with inaccurate flak and no fighter attacks. Still, it was eight hours in the air at 25,000 feet and 45 degrees below zero.

Freezing rain closed down the airfield for the remaining days of 1944 and the crew started a chess tournament with the cardboard sets they received as gifts in Bangor, Maine. Bert also managed to obtain a copy of Mark Twain's *Life on the Mississippi*, which helped to keep his mind off the danger ahead.

Though it arrived several weeks late, a Christmas Eve letter from Mary Jane must have improved his morale.

> December 23, 1944
> Every time I feel lonesome I always seem to turn to you. The reason isn't clear to me unless it's because of the many happy hours we've spent together. Although I have never been able to say I love you, I do know that I am pretty fond of you.... Last night I was feeling a little blue, so as usual, I thought of you and wrote a short letter.... If all the gang were here, they'd be planning a sleigh ride. Can't you just see them all?... "I Dream of You" is playing on the radio. Songs always seem to hit the thought of the moment lately. I don't think I'll ever get tired of dreaming about you and all our memories.

CHAPTER 13

"Hit 'em Good Kid"

Fran spent the final months of 1944 on the opposite side of the globe crawling through the steaming jungles of the Philippines. I have no record of his experiences beyond a brief article in the Hartford Courant about his heroism in December 1944, but I have been able to track the movements of his unit and can, with some degree of certainty, describe what he encountered.

In October 1944, the 96th Infantry Division left Hawaii on warships bound for the Philippines. They invaded the island of Leyte on October 20 in an amphibious landing that began a battle that would last for two months and be one of the decisive operations in the Pacific War. Capturing the Philippines was crucial to establishing air and sea bases close enough to Japan to mount the final offensive. The Philippines also controlled sea routes to Borneo and Sumatra which supplied rubber and petroleum to Japan.

The battle began with the deafening thunder of American warships pounding the shoreline for nearly four hours. Plumes of black smoke rose from the beaches as hundreds of landing craft approached the shore around 10 a.m. Fran huddled behind the steel walls of his landing craft, terrified of the moment when its iron mouth would swing down and vomit soldiers into the surf. When the dreaded moment arrived, he waded toward the beach as Japanese artillery shells exploded all around him. The sounds were overwhelming: explosions, the swish of bullets slicing into the water just inches away, and the groans of fellow soldiers as they were hit and collapsed into the waves.

Fran's first taste of combat was the October 20, 1944 invasion of Leyte in the Philippines, a blooding landing that was reminiscent of D-Day. (United States Coast Guard, Wikimedia Commons)

He made it to shore, but then had to cross 100 yards of open land to the swamps that separated the beach from the hills beyond. Some men nearly drowned under the weight of their packs as they sank into the marshes. Ahead of them, heavy artillery fire from the ships pounded the land behind the swamps as terrified Philippine children and adults ran for cover. They spent the next three days advancing through knee-deep rice paddies, discarding food and equipment to lighten their load on the 15-mile march.

The 96th had a reputation for marksmanship that earned it the nickname "the Deadeye Division." Fran had excelled in this regard and became his squad's "BAR man." The BAR (Browning Automatic Rifle) was a rifle-shaped machine gun that fired 20-round clips. The gun alone weighed 80 pounds, and ammunition made the burden even greater. So as the 383rd Infantry Regiment slogged through the swamps behind the beach, Fran was carrying more than his share of the load.

The BAR man often took the point position during patrols, which meant that Fran was most likely the lead soldier as his squad slogged through swamps and into the mountainous terrain where the Japanese lay in wait.

Their first task was to take Catmon Hill, a 1,400-foot promontory that towered over the beaches just north of where they landed. The Japanese had fortified the hill with heavy artillery and pillboxes. As the American forces worked their way up through the dense vegetation, they were frequently ambushed by Japanese soldiers hidden in the caves that are common on those volcanic islands. By the time they took the hill after 11 days of heavy fighting, they had cleared 17 caves, 53 pillboxes, and numerous heavy artillery emplacements. That must have been a terrifying assignment.

But the battle had just begun. It would take more than two months to secure the island. From Catmon Hill, Fran's unit moved into the mountainous jungles to cut enemy supply lines. On November 8, the monsoons began, flooding the trenches where Fran slept and turning roads into rivers of muck. Mudslides paralyzed American trucks and supplies were carted through the hills on bamboo stretchers carried by the Philippine islanders who were helping to liberate their country.

The fierce fighting and relentless rains made life miserable for ordinary grunts like Francis A. Brighenti. In the midst of this misery, some night in mid-December, Fran's unit was ambushed by enemy fire. Mortar shells rained down around them and machine-gun fire had them pinned. Fran spotted a flash 125 yards away, set his BAR on its tripod, and waited for a second flash. When the enemy fired another mortar shell, he silenced the assault with several bursts from his BAR.

Suddenly, the world around them was quiet. They approached the gun emplacement carefully and found three dead Japanese fighters. Fran received a ribbon for his valor and a write-up in his hometown newspaper back in Hartford.

By Christmas, American forces had largely secured Leyte and by New Year's Day, Private Brighenti was resting in an Army base behind the fighting where he could lay down his BAR and take up his pen.

> January 1, 1945:
> Happy New Year Bert.
>
> What do you think of Italy? You'll probably say, "Not much," but you should see the Philippines. Right now, the rainy season is starting to break, but when we got here it was in full swing. Rained

> every damn day, heavy and light. Lots of fun swimming in foxholes and waddling in swampy mud. But I'm used to it now and you can't have everything.
>
> Guess what? The Hartford Courant gave me a write-up for silencing a Jap mortar and three Nips. The clipping does a guy good, but I get plenty of ribbing about it.
>
> It happened one night when they did a counter-attack and I shot at a mortar flash with my BAR. They didn't fire anymore.
>
> We lived pretty roughly here for a couple of months in those muddy holes. However, things are now great, since we are in a post where we have Class B rations, movies, dry ground and PX facilities. Being New Year's Day we have a big turkey dinner on schedule for this afternoon and man do I like turkey.
>
> I take it you and little Miss Mary are fine and ever-loving.... Well Bert, I guess by the time this letter gets to you, you'll have quite a few bombing missions over Germany to your credit. Hit 'em good kid.

In all more than 3,000 American soldiers died on Leyte and another 15,000 were wounded. Fran was not among them. As he later wrote to Bert, he had survived the longest battle to date of the Pacific War "without a scratch."

★★★

The wars fought by Fran and Bert couldn't have been more different. Fran's war was up-front and personal. The enemy was often just a few dozen yards away. Fran could see their faces and they could see his. As the war progressed, the enemy would get even closer, sometimes so close it required hand-to-hand combat.

Bert's war was just as dangerous and just as terrifying, but it was a mechanized war. The flak guns were thousands of feet below, manned by Germans he could not see, and the fighter planes screamed out of the sky at 300 miles per hour with their cannons spitting strings of hot iron at them. He rarely caught a glimpse of the enemy pilots and never saw the flak gunners below who were determined to blow him into the past tense.

But there is another difference that's even more profound. Fran slept on the battlefield, often in mud-filled trenches knowing that the enemy could be creeping up on him at any minute.

For Bert, danger was confined to the eight-hour missions that consisted of seven hours of extreme discomfort and an hour or two of unimaginable violence. This all took place in an alien world of polar temperatures and depleted oxygen. They were also isolated from one another in quarters that made it almost impossible to move. These conditions posed a challenge to the human physiology which is programmed to respond to danger with a "fight or flight" response. Yet they could do neither. They had to wait for hours with nothing to do but clear the ice buildup from their oxygen lines until the world exploded around them and the entire universe seemed hell-bent on their destruction.

Still, if he survived the mission, Bert returned to a cot, a tent and dry blankets—and their makeshift stove. It was far from comfortable, but it was better than a flooded foxhole in the Philippines with the enemy crawling through the surrounding jungle. For Bert, the war was a series of nightmarish excursions into the apocalypse, but when he returned, he could exhale and begin the next chapter of Mark Twain's *Life on the Mississippi*. He could sleep knowing the Germans were hundreds of miles away.

CHAPTER 14

Too Close for Comfort

It snowed for three days, leading up to New Year's Day 1945. Bert and his crew spent the downtime finding ways to improve their chances of survival. One of those strategies was to interview fellow airmen who had to ditch their bombers in the ocean. Virtually all of their missions began and ended with several hours over the Adriatic Sea.

> Low fuel and/or damage to the plane could easily force a water landing. We practiced getting out of the plane as quickly as possible but practice is not the real thing and thus our eagerness to learn from those who had the real experience.

Not all of the lethal threats they endured occurred in the air. Two days later, one of the many dangers of life on the ground presented itself in dramatic fashion when one of the tents caught fire and burned down with everything in it.

> This is one of those situations in which the occupants of the tent decided to take a chance and keep the fire going all night in the interest of comfort. Luckily, no one died nor did the fire spread to adjacent tents—all with their 55 gallons of fuel next to their front doors.

For the airmen at Sterparone, their beloved stove was both a comfort and a constant danger. With this in mind, it was imperative that they keep the jury-rigged contraption in tip-top shape. On one day between missions, this required Bert to serve as ballast to keep the stove from rocketing through the roof of the tent.

Because of the imperfect burn of our aviation gasoline, soot built up in the chimney at a rapid rate. If the stovepipe was not cleaned, a chimney fire was inevitable. One could sit and watch a ring of red climb the pipe and keep one's fingers crossed in the hope that the canvass tent would not ignite. To forestall this, we had a weekly ritual in which one crew member was in charge of keeping the stove in the tent while another managed the explosion that blew all the soot out the top of the chimney. On this day, Ben [the tail gunner], was the blast master and I was the rocket launch suppressor, standing on top of the stove with a firm grip on the tent pole.

One thing we had learned about Ben was that, in certain situations, it was best to suggest that he do the opposite of what one wanted. In this instance, I forgot and said, "Ben, that's enough gas."

For a moment, the valve was turned full open. Ben then proceeded to the next step which was to light a long fuse of toilet paper and run to a safe distance. Which a huge bang, the stove and I went a third of the way up the tent pole.

Result: a very clean chimney.

Cleaning the stove: Even a mundane task like cleaning the stove could turn deadly since it required one crewman to light a gush of aircraft fuel while another stood on the stove to keep it from launching through the tent roof. (Frank Mullally)

★★★

It rained, it snowed, it sleeted, and in early January, a 65 mph gale destroyed a brick building and flattened several tents. It was miserable.

But misery wasn't the biggest problem posed by the unusual Italian weather. The Allied forces had created the Fifteenth Air Force and moved them to Italy for two reasons—geography and weather.

The German army needed planes and tanks and cannons, but they also needed fuel to operate those weapons as well as a transportation system to get the fuel where it was needed. The bulk of the Nazi oil supplies were located in eastern Europe, beyond the range of B-17s flying from England. One reason Allied forces invaded southern Italy in September 1943 was to establish air bases around Foggia. These bases, which were operational by early 1944, were a strategic milestone because the Axis oil fields of eastern Europe were 1,300 miles from England and only 600 air miles from Foggia. Score a big one for the good guys.

The weather, on the other hand, was far from a home run. English winters are known for their rain, fog, and constant cloud cover. But, ahhhh, what but sunny Italy? What perfect alternative to the gloomy British weather. The expectation was that the Fifteenth Air Force would be able to fly plenty of missions while the Eighth Air Force in England twiddled their thumbs waiting for a break in the cloud cover.

There are a few things you can count on in life, and one of them is that the weather will screw up the best laid plans, whether it's a vacation, a wedding, or a war. Sunny Italy was anything but sunny in the winter of 1944/45. In fact, the Eighth Air Force in England was able to fly 20 percent more often than the Fifteenth Air Force in Italy.

Despite this meteorological sucker punch, the Fifteenth Air Force played a crucial role in turning the tide in favor of Allied forces. This was possible due to the development of "Mickey Bombing," a term used for the new H2X ground mapping radar that made it possible to bomb accurately through heavy cloud cover from more than 25,000 feet.

So while the Eighth in England pounded German manufacturing plants in western Europe, the Fifteenth flew across the Alps to cripple the oil production and rail lines that transported fuel to the German tanks and aircraft.

Thanks to the Fifteenth Air Force in Italy, the Nazis were literally running out of gas.

★★★

Sometime before the New Year, Mary Jane sent Bert a letter that included the Hartford newspaper clipping about Fran's heroism. In a letter to his parents, he summed up the reaction of everyone who knew Fran:

> January 3, 1945
> Red sent a clipping about Fran Brighenti. He must have done quite a job on Leyte. That guy's getting too close to the enemy for comfort.

On several occasions in the coming weeks and months, Bert and the enemy would get too close for comfort as well.

> **January 4, 1945**
> Verona, Italy. 26,000 ft. −43 degrees. 5,000 lbs. bombs … Shot at all the way from target to the coast. Caught flak in bomb bays. Casey almost out—anoxia.

While bombing the railroad yards outside Verona, Italy, they were attacked by the dreaded Messerschmitts. The German fighters swooped through their formation as the bombers approached their target and again on their return flight as they neared the Adriatic. But what caught Bert's attention was the heavy flak from below that pierced the bomb bay doors. To reduce the weight of the heavily armed B-17, designers made the plane's outer skin out of aluminum. This was strong from an engineering perspective, but when it came to flak and fighter attacks, the aluminum was like trying to stop a bullet with a skin of paper. There were isolated panels of armor positioned throughout the interior part of the plane—beneath the pilot's seat, along the bulkhead of the navigator's station, there was even a panel around the waist gunner's window—but in most areas of the plane, the crew was protected only by the aluminum outer skin. So when the flak came through the bomb bay doors on

Bert's third mission, it inspired him to bring along an extra flak helmet to place between his legs to protect the family jewels during the bomb runs—a precaution my brother and I appreciate to this day.

The comment on Casey is also instructive. As the ball turret gunner, he flew most of the eight-hour mission in a fetal position, sealed into a glass ball that hung underneath the plane. While the flak and fighters were terrifying, it was shifting his butt that almost got him killed. Because of the ever-present danger of anoxia, the pilots made announcements every 10 minutes for the crew to check their oxygen lines for icing. Casey shifted position right after one of those checks and accidently knocked loose his oxygen line. By the time the next oxygen check was announced, it would have been too late. Fortunately, he realized what had happened moments before he passed out and plugged his oxygen tube back in.

★★★

One of the things that perplex me about my father's retirement-age musings was that there are no reflections about the red-headed girl back home or why he was so certain he wanted to marry her. Nor did he describe the young men he flew with, even though he felt a lifelong devotion to these men and religiously attended bomber reunions around the country.

I think his generation's adherence to Hemingway's iceberg theory put handcuffs on a skilled writer who did not possess Hemingway's extraordinary aptitude for communicating powerful emotion through extreme understatement. Most of us have to actually say what we mean—and maybe even elaborate a bit—if we want others to understand.

The closest he came to capturing the personalities of the men he served with was in a letter he sent to his parents just after the new year.

> January 3, 1945
> Last night I was sitting here with Red's picture propped up against a can of foot powder. I had a trench knife supporting it. Frank asked me if it was a 5 × 7 photo and when I said "yes," he asked if he could borrow it because he had to measure something and

> we had no rulers. This morning, when I woke up, the picture was next to me in a frame that Frank had whittled out of scrap wood. Pretty decent of him, eh.

In this instance, his understatement was as powerful as he hoped it would be. Frank had cleverly disguised his kind intentions by pretending to need the 5 × 7 picture to measure something. The fruits of his efforts greeted my father when he opened his eyes in the morning. It was a simple gift between two men who repeatedly entered hell together and managed to emerge unharmed.

For Bert and many others, being an airman was only partly about fighting a war. Yes, he believed in the cause unconditionally, and yes, he was frightened during missions. He believed he had a job to do, and like every job he ever had—even working in a hammer factory between college semesters—Bert was determined to do it the best he possibly could. But most of all the war was about survival and the bond that formed among a group of randomly selected young men who had little in common beyond their tent, their plane, and their makeshift stove. Despite the terror and abject discomfort of the war, the most powerful emotion experienced by Bert's crew was a determination to never, under any circumstances, let their buddies down.

It's a pretty simple formula for life. It's a shame we need a war to make us live together that way.

CHAPTER 15

The Glass Ball

January 21, 1945

Vienna. 26,000 feet. 1,200 miles. Roughest mission yet. Flak very, very accurate. Several holes. One piece picked up in ammo box in radio room. Temp. −58 degrees. Almost froze to death in ball. Bends. Flak smoke split round ball. Two bomb runs, 50 minutes. Mickey bombing. 3 ships missing. One headed for Russia. Ben out—anoxia. One man froze to ball. 9 out of 10 ships hit in squadron. Our element leaders missing. Many frost bitten. 9 hours.

The "ball" Bert refers to is the ball turret. In the spirit of understanding the job of every crew member, Bert swapped positions with Casey on this mission and was flying in what had to be one of the most spectacular, terrifying, and bizarre positions for any soldier in any war.

> There is no question that the war looked different depending on where one was standing. This was true even though we were only a few feet apart. The best views of the action were from the bombardier's seat and the ball turret.

I doubt that the view was what impressed Bert most about this experience. The ball turret is a plexiglass and aluminum sphere, less than four feet in diameter, positioned on the bottom of the B-17 so that three quarters of the sphere is exposed. It was designed to be as small as possible to reduce drag, so there was just enough room for two large machine guns and a human folded nearly in half. The gunner climbed down into the ball from inside the plane feet first, slid into a fetal position, and locked

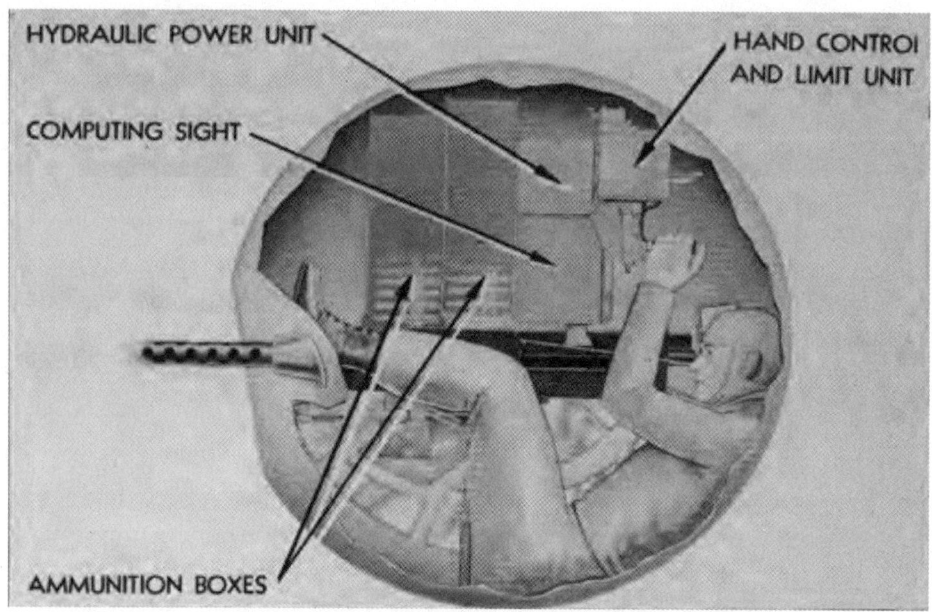

Ball turret gunners flew beneath the plane folded into a four-foot glass and aluminum egg. The quarters were so tight, there was no room for a parachute. (*Handbook of Instructions for Lower Ball Turrets*)

the door above himself. Then he rotated the ball so he was lying on his back parallel to the ground, with his feet in the air at the same height as his head. He was now looking through a gunsight that was positioned between his feet. His job was to protect the underside of the plane from enemy fighters and he had controls that could rotate the ball 360 degrees in the horizontal and 90 degrees in the vertical.

There was no room for a parachute, so if an emergency occurred, the gunner had to hope there was time to rotate the ball, unlock the door above, climb out, and grab his chute, which was hanging in the main fuselage. If the hydraulics were damaged by enemy fire, he was trapped in that hamster ball and had to pray that his crewmates had time to rotate the ball manually from inside the plane. But when a B-17 was in a fiery death spiral, there wasn't much time, so many ball turret gunners went down with the aircraft. This was one reason the mortality rate among ball turret gunners was double that of other crew members. This was not a comforting thought as Bert headed into a flak barrage.

The view was, indeed, spectacular, though it did leave a person feeling a tad exposed. The 360-degree panorama included flak exploding all around and enemy fighter planes racing at you with their cannons firing. Ball turret gunners were known to get shot right out of their see-through eggshell and fall to their deaths.

The day Bert flew in the ball, they had to make two runs at the target—a railway repair yard in Vienna—which extended the time without heat from 20 minutes to 50 minutes. That's a long time at 58 degrees below zero. So Bert wasn't exaggerating when he wrote, "Almost froze to death in the ball" in his wartime diary. He also experienced the bends, an excruciating pain in his knees caused by nitrogen buildup in the blood while at 26,000 feet. In another plane on the same mission, the ball turret gunner froze to the side of the ball and lost an ear.

On this mission, the dense cloud cover forced them to abort the first bomb run and fly the entire formation in a 360-degree turn so they could make a second run at the target. As they approached the target a second time, the Germans unleashed a barrage of flak, some of which narrowly missed the ball.

> One could watch each burst come closer to the nose of the plane and then, with a slight momentary lift of a wing, the fourth burst would be slightly off to the side. Sometimes, the fourth burst would be far enough ahead that there would be no evasive action and the smoke from the explosion would split around the ball. Interesting!

In his retirement-age recollections, Bert described the ball as a "rather lonely and isolated spot." I suspect that was a bit of an understatement. It was a brutal mission, with nine of the 10 planes in his squadron hit, including his own. When they were finally back over Italy it was snowing again. The visibility was so bad they had to come down over Foggia on the coast and follow the telephone lines back to the Sterparone airfield. According to Bert, they lost 17 bombers during that mission.

Bert's diary entry for the next day tersely states, "Santiago missing on Vienna raid." We never learn who Santiago was or what Bert felt about the 17 missing bombers. Instead, his reflections include an extended description of learning to play poker from a pair of card sharps on the base.

★★★

With a little research, I was able to fill in some of the gaps. Juan Santiago was the bombardier on a plane piloted by Victor Prescott. The entire crew was listed as missing in action after their plane was hit during the Vienna mission. They lost two of their four engines, and were last seen limping eastward toward the Russian lines.

They barely made it. The plane—which was the same plane that Bert crewed on two weeks earlier over Verona—crash-landed in southern Hungary just behind the Russian lines. Prescott must have been a very good pilot because he landed the disabled plane in a field without a single death. Army records show that Prescott, Santiago, and the rest of the crew were rescued by Hungarian civilians who delivered them to Russian troops. Three weeks later, on February 13, Bert noted in his wartime diary that Prescott and his crew arrived back at the Sterparone air base ready to resume their fight against Germany. I don't know what became of Santiago, but an obituary states that Victor Prescott survived the war, had a family, and died at the age of 91 in Washington State.

Because being shot down was a constant danger, all airmen were provided with fake papers that included a photograph of themselves unshaven and wearing peasant clothes. The hope was that they would be able to pass as locals while making their way back toward Allied lines. They also received capture-avoidance training. Among the interesting tidbits of information they received was that if they were shot down over Vienna, they should take the #10 bus to the end of the line, where they would find a foreign workers' camp that would provide temporary shelter.

I wonder if anyone who parachuted out of those 17 downed bombers that day were able to catch the #10 bus.

★★★

January 1945 ended with a bang. Literally. Fortunately for Bert, he was in his tent rather than at the airfield at the time.

On some missions, bombs got jammed and wouldn't release. In most cases, the crew was able to kick the bombs loose over the Adriatic on the return flight. But occasionally a few stubborn bombs just wouldn't let go. This was a problem because there was always a chance that the impact of landing would detonate a jammed bomb. This is what happened on January 31, 1945. The explosion shook Bert in his tent a mile away, blew a gaping hole in the runway, and killed both the waist gunner and radio man. Bert saw the plane two days later and there was still blood all over the radio room. They washed it out with a firehose.

There are so many inglorious ways to get killed in a war.

★★★

While Bert was dodging flak over Austria, Fran was living in relative comfort on the tropical island of Leyte. He had exchanged his flooded foxhole for a tent in the mountains, which were now under Allied control. He used the time to write letters to his buddies and think about the future.

> February 5, 1945
> What's new in spaghetti land fella? It was swell to hear from you yesterday. Things have been going fine in the Philippines since I last wrote. We cleaned up the yellow bastards in the mountains a few weeks ago and now we live ala garrison doing MP duty on the highways here to keep busy. We have a damn nice company area, put some work into it, and really fixed up a nice spot. The tents are right beside a clear river under palm trees and we have movies every night....
>
> It was damn good to hear that your rival is upon foreign shores. Makes the home front safe, also gives the woman time to think things over. With me, Cupid still keeps me and that Kentucky belle happy. It even looks like I'll be bringing a newcomer to old Connecticut.
>
> Hey Bert, how about letting me in on some of your postwar plans, and don't give me that line that you haven't got any, because I know damn well that every guy overseas thinks about what the

hell he's going to do when he gets back in the great US again. As I remember, you were planning on going back to Dartmouth, but what I want to know is what business you're heading for. What's it going to be, run a nightclub, movies, theater, engineering, sales, science, teaching? You don't have to guess what I'm heading for. Man, I have more angles for the construction business, and with a little help from the West Hartford Trust, a few projects are going to pop up around Connecticut. I also plan to throw all my college credits from the Army together and see if I can get my degree in two years....

I'm glad you like my publicist, but I had nothing to do with it. What a heckling I'm going to get when the boys read it. It was terrific to get a ribbon, but the ribbon I'd really like to get is the great Pabst Blue Ribbon.

All the talk about Bert's post-war business plans surprised me a bit until I remembered that after the war, he was accepted to an MBA program at Dartmouth's Tuck School for Business Administration. It's a good thing he chose not to go. He was a first-rate psychologist, but a lousy businessman. We all would have starved.

During those days of rest, Fran also wrote one of several letters to Bert's mother. In many ways, Hartford was still a small town in 1945. It was the kind of place where high school kids knew their friends' parents as well as they knew their own aunts and uncles. Bert's father often ran into Mary Jane walking to the bus stop and gave her a ride to work. Mary Jane ran into Bert's younger sister and sent him news about his kid sister's junior year in high school. Before the war, Fran spent countless hours in Bert's kitchen or backyard, and Bert did the same at Fran's house. So it's not all that surprising that when he had a few peaceful moments away from the fighting, he thought of the people back home.

February 23, 1945
Dear Mom Ibelle:

I guess the three buddies [Bert, Fran and Bob] are all pitching in now but we are really waiting for the day that we can pitch in back in Hartford again in those grand old times at home and at

> the shore. Just fond memories a fella can't forget and wants to do again. We are resting in garrison now beside a clear river lined by palm trees. The rainy season has quit and it means warm sunny days like summer back home. The nights are cool and believe it or not, we aren't bothered by mosquitoes.... I see that you folks are getting a visit from Old Man Winter this year with snow and more snow. I could go for a little sleigh riding right now, though I would look funny on Hartford streets with the tan I have from the tropical sun.... I know Mr. Ibelle, or would he rather I call him Howard, still has plenty of smiles and the pep to go with them. I want him to pick me out a nice car when I get home because the old gang isn't planning on walking after being in the Army.... Bob and I will be 21 come May—turning into young men aren't we? Won't be long before we plan to start homes, though there will be a couple of years of study and playtime before that.

Like Mary Jane's frequent references to "the good old days," Fran longed for the simpler more innocent world he had lived in just a short time ago. Nostalgia at such a young age is striking, but hardly surprising given their circumstances. Fran was dreaming of the day when he could cast off the horrors of war and return to the world he once knew where people treated each other with kindness, affection, and hope for the future.

★★★

While Fran was enjoying his well-deserved rest in the Philippines, Bert was in the thick of it on the other side of the globe. During their fifth mission on February 7, they encountered heavy flak while bombing oil refineries outside Vienna, one of the most heavily fortified cities in Nazi territory. Bert's plane was riddled with holes, including one just inches above his head.

They were flying plane #327 for the third time. They would fly this plane on a total of seven missions and considered it their lucky plane. They were right—but it wasn't until the final month of the war that Bert learned that it was his lucky plane for a reason he never imagined.

In his diary entry the next day, Bert notes that their bomber group had missed the target by three miles and unloaded 5,000 pounds of explosives on Vienna itself, rather than the oil refinery. The problem was that German flak guns had knocked out their radar (the Mickey bombing equipment), so with thick cloud cover beneath them, they had to rely on manual calculations to pinpoint the target. In his retirement-age reflections, Bert says nothing about accidentally dropping two-and-a-half tons of explosives on the people of Vienna.

During their next mission, a B-17 in their group blew up when it was hit by a bomb dropped by a plane above. Two days later, they flew their seventh mission on a plane that was shot down a month later over Vienna. This was starting to become a pattern.

Their target on that mission was a Benzine plant in Linz, Austria, but they had to turn back when their pilot passed out over the Alps. Bert noted that they were lucky because the incident occurred just minutes before the arrival of German fighters, which often trailed the bomber groups looking for stragglers that would be easy targets.

> Yesterday, we were extremely lucky that we pulled out of formation when we did. It would not have been fun to play tag with four fighters that were determined to make us "It."

CHAPTER 16

Anatomy of a Mission

H-hour arrived at 3 a.m. with a loud banging of pots, which got closer as the human alarm clock paraded along the line of tents. Each mission began with two daunting tasks that had nothing to do with enemy fire: getting off the ground and dressing for the show. The struggle began with the first layer of clothing: summer underwear, long johns, winter jumpsuit, socks, shoes, scarf, winter flight jacket, knit hat.

Breakfast was minimal. Although it would be 14 hours before they ate again, they dined on nothing but black coffee and dry toast because they didn't want to eat anything that would produce intestinal gas. As Bert noted, "at 30,000 feet, a thimble of gas would expand to the point where you felt as if you were giving birth to a watermelon."

Although these were rational men doing a job that they knew depended on knowledge, skill, and teamwork, superstitions were common among bomber crews.

> Of course, none of our crew cottoned to such nonsense. It was just a habit that one of our crew always stuck a well-chewed wad of gum outside his cockpit window, another made sure he wore the same underwear on each mission, and that on leaving the briefing room, the four gunners aft of the radio room always walked under a ladder that perpetually leaned against the wall of headquarters. Thus we showed our utter contempt for such folderol. It was only the most gross of coincidences that the one time we did not perform this counterphobic maneuver, we got the hell kicked out of us.

The hour after briefing was a time of mounting anxiety. They hustled out into the January darkness and hopped on the back of a flatbed truck which drove them through the pre-dawn chill to the airstrip, where they would prepare the plane.

As the crew's gunnery expert, Bert inspected the bomb load, the ammunition boxes, and each of the 13 machine guns. Each man worked with concentrated efficiency to complete his task. Then they waited. And waited.

Eventually a flare would go up—Green = start your engines; Yellow = keep waiting; Red = mission canceled. No one wanted to see a red flare at this point. They had done all the mental and physical work to prepare for the mission and cancellation would only lead to more frustration, anxiety, and boredom.

On this day, February 15, they got a green flare for their sixth mission, so the pilots started their four engines one at a time. The propeller spun slowly at first as the engine fired mini explosions, each followed by a puff of smoke out the exhaust. As the propeller gained speed, the explosions and puffs quickened like an old-fashioned choo-choo train building speed until the firing pistons blurred together into the unmistakable hum of a B-17. It was Bert's job to stand behind the engines with a fire extinguisher in case one caught fire.

Takeoff was always an adventure. With 5,000 pounds of bombs as payload, the "Flying Fortress" looked like a cormorant struggling to take flight after leaping from a rock. The runway at Sterparone was barely long enough for the massive bombers so to compensate for this, pilots inched their planes onto the furthest end of the runway, pressed down the brake pedal with all their weight, and revved the engines to full throttle before releasing the brakes. The plane gathered speed gradually—far too gradually for Bert's liking. It seemed like he could run to the end of the runway faster than the lumbering bomber could get there. But somehow, moments before it reached the end, the pilot pulled back on the yoke and the landing gear lifted off the ground—one foot, then two feet, then three feet. Shit, we're going to fly right into that stone barn!

Still, without sufficient lift, the pilot turned the plane slightly to avoid taking the roof of that barn, then dropped the plane into a shallow valley just beyond the first line of stone walls. The brief descent gave the plane enough airspeed for the pilot to pull back on the controls and muscle the bomber and its 5,000 pounds of explosives above the countryside.

Bert likened the procedure to an aircraft carrier takeoff where the fighters accelerate across the deck and when they cross the bow of the ship, drop towards the ocean to build airspeed before turning skyward. It was an exhilarating way to begin every mission, but I'm sure all those involved would have appreciated a few hundred feet of additional runway.

On this day, the squadron had to climb through thick clouds as they maneuvered into formation.

> The clouds were so dense that one could see only the wing tip of the plane to the side and catch a slight glimpse of the tail of the plane ahead. We were flying "in the hole," which meant that we had three planes above and to the front, a plane on each wing, and three planes below and behind. At the same time, squadrons and groups were jockeying for position in this cloud-blinded world.
>
> We eventually broke into the clear. It was an awesome sight to watch hundreds and hundreds of bombers boil up out of the clouds, for all the world like Japanese beetles in August.

Once they were above the cloud cover, Bert inched out onto the catwalk that spanned the bomb bay to pull the pins out of the bombs. To get to the last set of pins, he had to lower himself down and spread-eagling the catwalk so he could bend double and reach down to the lowest set of bombs. He had to perform this high-wire act without a parachute because there was no room for this gear in the bomb bay.

Once they tested each of the machine guns, it was time to wrestle with the next layer of clothing. They performed this sartorial ballet as quickly as possible because the temperature was now well below zero as they continued to gain altitude. The first move was to take off their flight jacket, which encouraged the rapid completion of the dance:

1. Climb into heated suit and fleece-lined winter flying pants.
2. Put on flight jacket.
3. Wrestle self into parachute harness.
4. Remove walking boots and wire them to the parachute harness in case they have to abandon the plane.
5. Slide freezing feet into heated booties and fleece-lined boots.
6. Yank on silk gloves liners followed by fleece-lined gloves.
7. Put on the "Mae West" life preserver over the parachute harness.

8. Put on knit hat followed by a fleece-lined flying helmet with earphones.
9. Secure oxygen mask with microphone.
10. Put on tinted goggles.

While all this was taking place, the pilots gradually gained altitude and began forming up into the designated combat formation. It took about 40 minutes for a loaded B-17 to reach 20,000 feet and an hour to gather together all the planes into a tight formation. The basic unit of the formation was the squadron of 9–12 planes that flew in a tight 3-dimensional "combat box" designed to do two things: 1) maximize defensive firepower by ensuring that all guns could be fired without hitting other bombers in the formation, and 2) allow all planes to drop their bombs without hitting other bombers. Although the formations varied in size and pattern from mission to mission, each pattern required planes to fly extremely close together and maintain the pattern for hundreds

Bert on his way to 29,000 feet. (The Ibelle family)

of miles. Flying in 12-plane squadrons in tight formation for six hours or more required an enormous amount of skill and concentration on the part of the pilots.

After more than three hours in the air, they were finally approaching their bomb run. They were now at 29,000 feet with temperatures hovering around 40 below zero. It was time for the final movement of the ballet.

Step 1: Attach the parachute to its harness "so it would leave the plane with us if we got blown out."

Step 2: Put on the flak jacket, a long parka of overlapping metal plates that hung just below the groin, front and back, and weighed 16 pounds.

Step 3: Now that they were sufficiently burdened with gear for warmth and safety, they put on their steel flight helmet and strapped a Colt 45 to their belt in case things didn't go well and they had to bail out behind enemy lines (hoping to find the #10 bus of course).

The defensive "combat box" formation required pilots to fly hundreds of miles just a few dozen yards apart. (United States Army Air Forces)

Finally … all dressed and ready for the dance. (Frank Mullally)

Step 4: Stuff every pocket with K-rations, cigarettes, chocolate bars, and any other item that might be useful for survival or barter in case the plane went down and they found themselves on an unplanned walkabout in Nazi-occupied Europe.

"At this point," wrote Bert, "we were properly attired to join the party."

But their discomfort was still not complete. As the German flak guns started pumping explosives into their path, the pilot gave the order to disconnect all heated suits and gun heaters so the plane would have maximum power during the bomb run. That meant an average of 20 minutes without heat. In the waist gunner position, Bert had the added pleasure of the sub-zero wind coming from the open bomb bay doors. It was the moment of truth:

> The bombardier would announce "Bombs Away," a bit of information that was hardly necessary since the plane would surge upward as it shed two-and-a-half tons in a matter of seconds.

With the bombs released, the formation banked a 180-degree turn and headed for home. If they made it through the Nazi curtain-call of flak and Messerschmitts, they were rewarded back at the base with coffee, donuts, a debriefing session, and finally "a liberal ration of medicinal whiskey that made life seem worth living."

★★★

It was about this time that Bert received a letter from Mary Jane in which she tried to explain her reluctance to say the three words Bert wanted to hear. It must have been reassuring on one hand and frustrating on the other. It also must have further convinced him that, in addition to being pretty and fun, Mary Jane was the type of deeply considerate person who was worthy of his unwavering devotion.

> February 12, 1945
> Dear Bert:
>
> I'm going to attempt to explain what I meant when I said "If I didn't think so much of you, I could say 'I love you'" and take the chance that I'd feel the same when you come back. Perhaps when you do come back, I can say it and know that I really mean it. You know that I'm not very good at writing, so try very carefully to understand.
>
> At the time you left school to go into the Army, I thought it was Bill that I loved. You weren't home for 1½ years and then you came home and that Saturday night became one of our memories. I felt that maybe I could love you, but I wasn't sure. I knew you were going over then, and I didn't know how much that had to do with my feelings. Lots of girls feel that way when fellows are leaving. That's why so many wartime marriages go wrong. Their love was only temporary. I don't want to hurt you the way many of these young people are likely to hurt each other. That's what I meant when I said that in my letter. I think too much of you to do that.
>
> I hope that I have helped you a little with my attempt at explaining. I'll never say I love anyone again until I am positive. You and Bill were after me to make a decision once, but I won't say it again until it's to my future husband. I swear by all that is holy that I will do just what I said even if I end up being an old maid. So you can be sure that when I say those three words it will be the truth. I pray to God that I am doing the right thing when I put this letter into the mailbox.

Two days later, Mary Jane sent another letter to Bert, congratulating him on his promotion to sergeant and noting that the moonlight was shining on the snow outside her window—a perfect night for one of their sleigh rides around Goodwin Park. "A Little on the Lonely Side" was playing on the radio and, golly, that was the song for her at the moment.

Throughout March, her letters kept coming in a flurry. Judging from the tone of those letters, two of Bert's most dominant qualities—patience and persistence—were paying off.

> March 9, 1945
> … It means a lot to me that you understood my last letter. Lots of fellows would have told me off a long time ago, and certainly after that letter. Sometimes I wonder why you never have. I really don't deserve it but I'm glad you think I do. Golly, you're tops.

> March 10, 1945
> … It is Saturday night and a very dreary night at that. It was raining, but has turned to snow. I guess I'm in tune with the weather—just little low and blue. As always, I seem to turn to you because I always feel a little better after "talking" with you.

> March 15, 1945
> … I can see us running down Washington Street that night we went bowling. We certainly must have looked crazy.

Bert must have sensed that the tide was turning in his favor because he was confident enough to report his optimism in a letter to his parents.

> March 23, 1945
> Dear Folks:
> …. I've been getting quite a few letters from Red and things are looking pretty good. She sure is a swell kid.

CHAPTER 17

The Little Box of Horrors

February 20, 1945

Vienna oil refineries. We will never live to tell of flak that comes closer. We heard every explosion. One knocked me 3 inches off the floor. 5 hurt. 1 killed. Several shot down.

Vienna had 640 flak cannons in place at the time, which included perimeter installations, mobile guns mounted on rail cars, and a series of impervious flak towers constructed in the heart of the city that survive to this day. Bert would fly a total of seven missions into the meat grinder known as Vienna and statistics show that a third of the bombers that flew missions over the city suffered heavy damage.

Bert saw many B-17s explode in flames like this one, which was shot down over Yugoslavia in April 1944. (US Air Force)

As the bombers approached the city, the sky erupted with a fireworks finale that had only one purpose. Bert watched one bomber spin downward leaving a trail of black smoke before it exploded midair.

So many planes were shot down or suffered heavy damage on the February 20 mission that their next mission had to be canceled because only 20 of the group's 75 planes were operational. In an amazing display of efficiency, American repair crews had the bulk of those planes ready by the end of the week. In the meantime, Bert was appointed as gunnery instructor, a job that required him to fly extra practice missions to train new crews. He was also able to score one of the most prized possessions among airmen at the time—a new pair of shoes.

> Obtaining shoes was always a pleasure. With the constant exposure to wet and muck, they rotted right off your feet and it wasn't unusual for your feet to rot right along with them. The battle of Gettysburg was fought for shoes and one of the main reasons the South lost the war was the inability to keep their soldiers well shod. At least we occasionally got replacements.

On February 27, they were airborne again, bombing the train depot at Augsburg, Germany, where heavy flak explosions lifted Bert off the floor several times. He described the explosions as "a dull WHOOMP followed by a SHHH-shhhh as though someone was throwing gravel at the plane." That was the sound of hot metal showering the fuselage of the plane. The shrapnel shattered the top turret, punctured the extra fuel tank, and barely missed Frank's head in the radio room.

> I noticed that from that time on, Frank wore his flak helmet—something he had not done before. Frank had a lot of faith, but he also believed in lending a helping hand when the good Lord nudged him a bit.

During the bomb drop, Bert saw three B-17s get hit and spin toward the earth in flames as only five parachutes appeared below them. One can only imagine what it was like dangling from a parachute as the bombers above released a diarrhea of 500-pound bombs. His own plane was shot up badly and they finished the mission with holes in all four engines. It seemed like death was clawing closer to him with every mission.

In early March, Bert had four missions in rapid succession over Germany, Austria, and Hungary—three of them aboard their lucky plane #327. While flying over friendly territory on the second of these missions, the news came over Armed Forces radio that President Roosevelt had assured the mothers of America that there were no 19-year-olds flying in combat.

> Ben, who was the only member of the crew younger than me, immediately got on the intercom: "Guys, I just found out that I'm not here. The President said so. If I'm not here, then you can't be here. That means that the Krauts can't do anything to us."

On the last of this string of missions, another plane my father had recently flown in—"The Old Shillalah"—was shot down on a mission to Vienna. After bombs away, while turning for home, it took a direct hit and lost two of its four engines. The pilot made a run for the Russian front, losing altitude steadily until he had to make a wheels-up landing in a field just behind the Russian lines. There were no serious injuries and the entire crew eventually made it back to the Sterparone air base.

It was yet another plane Bert had recently flown in, lost in another crash-landing.

On that same March 16 mission, Bert suffered a horror that was more grotesque than deadly. Although the flak was quite heavy over the Vienna railway yards, it was not the type of explosives that caused the biggest problem. The crew had been served tainted food the previous night and the resulting intestinal ailments became much worse at altitude, forcing them to strip off a half dozen layers of clothes and equipment in sub-zero conditions. If vomiting was involved, the oxygen mask had to be removed at well-timed moments and replaced before the nauseous airman passed out. Bert and Gene, the two waist gunners, had to perform this operation for Ben when he was vomiting on a previous mission, putting his oxygen mask on and off quickly as he expelled the contents of his stomach.

On this mission, most of the crew was affected, so they improvised a toilet out of an ammo box, which they placed in the radio room. The trouble came when a piece of shrapnel punctured the box, causing a foul stream to leak under the radio room door and get caught in the wind coming around the ball turret. Opening the bomb bay doors turbo-charged the atomization. At age 68, Bert took a pre-adolescent glee in describing the situation:

> I have always suspected that Gene and I shared the rare distinction of being shit on, pissed on, and puked on all at the same time. I wonder if Guinness [World Records] would be interested.

My father's uncharacteristic bathroom humor provides further evidence that boys will be boys, even when they're 68-year-old men.

CHAPTER 18

The Angels Sing

March 20, 1945

Vienna, Austria. Target: Kagran oil refineries. Altitude 28,500. Burst #2 knocked out my window, gun, oxygen, rudder controls, heated suit—hit me. Smashed everything in the waist. Two holes over my head 6 inches and 12 inches across. Multi smaller holes. Ben hit. Chin turret out. Ball turret out. Autopilot out. Interphone out. Oxygen gone in seconds. Peeled off and dove to 15,000 feet. All the way back alone. Hit three times by flak. Lost multi planes. Ambulance waiting for Ben and I at hard stand.

As they approached the final bomb run, the German flak guns filled the sky with hundreds of black and white explosions that sent ragged shards of shrapnel in every direction. Bert's plane was hit and disabled immediately. So was Bert.

He wrote that it felt as though he had been clubbed from behind with a baseball bat. He fell to his knees, momentarily passed out, and as he regained consciousness, he heard a high-pitched whistle and thought it was the angels singing in heaven.

Fortunately, it was not. He quickly realized that the singing was the sound of the air whistling out of his severed oxygen line. This presented a problem of its own since he could only last about a minute without oxygen. But that wasn't the only problem. The shrapnel had also disabled the plane's power supply, which meant two things: 1) their heated suits no longer worked, and 2) Casey was trapped in the ball turret.

> I was brought back to my senses by a powerful boot in the rear by Gene [the other waist gunner] who was desperately trying to crank up the ball turret so that Casey could get out.

Bert grabbed an emergency oxygen canister and they passed the mask between them as they cranked. Once Casey was out of the ball, the crew lined up around the bomb bay doors ready to bail out. Bert got Ben's attention in the isolated the tail gunner position by throwing empty shell casings at him and motioning him forward. He had been hit in the left arm. Seconds before they jumped, the top turret gunner relayed a message from the pilot to stay put.

> That was when we made our rapid descent to 15,000 feet. We dropped the first 1,000 feet in 45 seconds.

The motor for the bomb bay doors had been disabled by the flak, so once they were flying level again, Bert went forward to hand-crank them closed, a process that required about 100 turns at 15,000 feet with no oxygen.

Flak blew out Bert's window, hit him in the shoulder, and knocked him unconscious. (The Ibelle family)

They were alive and still flying, but their troubles were far from over. With the communication out, the pilot couldn't talk with the navigator, Dick Swears, which caused them to drift towards the Russian front where another round of Nazi flak knocked out the top turret. Fortunately, the gunner, Lou Morehouse, had just gone forward to speak with the pilot and wasn't present when the blast wiped out his position. Not long after this, they passed over an airfield at Wels, Austria, and got slammed with a third round of flak that bounced the plane and took out the chin turret. The final round of flak came from rail guns positioned somewhere near the Alps.

> Although by this time we were more than a bit weary of the whole business, we had one more encounter. This time with a rail gun. Gene and I wound up on the floor with our arms wrapped around each other.

The final challenge came as they approached their home base and discovered that the shrapnel had cut off power to the landing gear. So as they approached the coast of Italy, they took turns hand-cranking the landing gear into position.

Never had the screech and bounce of wheels on the runway sounded so good. There was an ambulance waiting on the runway for Bert and Ben. When the flight surgeon examined them at the field hospital, he discovered multiple cuts and burns and ordered them to remain in the hospital overnight for observation. The two airmen objected, saying they had to attend a critical debriefing for the mission. When their pleas were rejected, they told the flight surgeon—aptly named Dr. Argue—that they had spotted two camouflaged airfields that were not on the charts and that they suspected these were bases for the new German jet fighter planes. Based on this assertion, Dr. Argue sent them to the debriefing in an ambulance, which he ordered to wait and return them to the medical tent as soon as the meeting concluded.

> Our real reasons for wanting to attend the debriefing had nothing to do with the fictitious airfields. Reason #1 involved the Salvation Army's coffee and doughnuts. We had nothing to eat for the past 12 hours. We had been cold, tense, and on oxygen for the last six hours. The ladies met us with a trash barrel full of steaming hot, rich, black coffee and a couple of the crispiest, tastiest doughnuts one could wish for.

> Our second reason was to line up for the post-mission ration of medicinal whiskey. This was a couple ounces served in a tin measuring cup. Ben and I drained ours and were headed for the door when the medic called us back saying, "You guys need more than that." He then proceeded to fill the cups, Ben and I dutifully disposed of the extra ration. After all, it was not wise to ignore a medical order. We then went to the debriefing and by the time we were ready to return to the infirmary, we had a pressing need for the ambulance.

When Bert and Ben arrived back at the medical tent, Dr. Argue was furious because they were too drunk to send them to Foggia for X-rays without risking court-martial himself.

> Thus, we had our fourth ambulance ride of the day and, in compliance with Doc Argue's instructions, we both had a most sound and refreshing sleep.

The next day, they went out to examine the damage to their plane, which they found in the junkyard, riddled with holes. Despite the beating they had taken, theirs wasn't the plane with the worst damage. One of the B-17s made it back with a hole the size of a horse in its side, thus reinforcing their belief that the B-17 was a remarkably resilient aircraft.

Both Bert and Ben received the Purple Heart for their injuries and the pilot, Ted Frink, received a Distinguished Flying Cross for saving all of their lives.

Bert Ibelle (lower right) in one of the planes that somehow made it back to the Sterparone airbase—demonstrating the remarkable durability of B-17s. (The Ibelle family)

CHAPTER 19

The Isolation Room

My father kept a small leather box hidden among the socks in his bureau drawer. The box contained his Purple Heart and one of the pieces of shrapnel that hit him. The piece he saved was a three-inch piece of twisted metal that was pulled out of his flak jacket. (The doctor didn't save any of the smaller shards pulled from his back.) When we were boys, my brother and I would sneak into our parents' bedroom and pull the case out to marvel at the Purple Heart and try to imagine what it must have been like to have angry pieces of hot metal come screaming through the sky, puncture the plane, and then slam into your back.

Bert won the Purple Heart for his injuries during the March 20, 1945 mission over Vienna. It is seen here along with a 3-inch piece of metal they pulled out of his flight jacket. (The shrapnel the doctor pulled out of his shoulder was not saved.) (The Ibelle family)

My father wasn't the kind of dad who was your best buddy. He didn't teach us how to shoot a basketball or fix a car engine. But we were proud of his Purple Heart. We were also proud that he ran the psychiatric ward at Hartford Hospital. Both were mysterious and exotic. We knew his job was important and secretly felt important ourselves whenever we were out to dinner and Dr. Ibelle was paged about an emergency on the psych ward. He couldn't talk about his work because of confidentiality issues, so like the war, his professional life remained a mystery.

The summer after my freshman year in college, I decided to investigate that mystery by getting a job as an aide on the ward that he ran. For me, it was an opportunity to satisfy two urges that burned in my adolescent brain—find out more about my father, and explore a nightmarish slice of the world that was strictly off limits to the general public.

I felt surprisingly comfortable in the unsettled world of CCU2 (Continuing Care Unit, second floor). I was fascinated by the people who landed there and, even though I was just 18 years old, I had an ability to remain calm and reassuring to patients who were in the thrall of despair or psychosis. I was surprised to find that most of the patients were not crazy in the Hollywood sense of the word. They were just people with problems—big problems for sure—but for the most part, their peculiarities of thought and style didn't seem all that different from the people I knew in regular life; just more so.

As for my father, I saw a calm, competent man who wielded his authority with infinite kindness, both toward the patients and his staff. I never had the opportunity to see him doing therapy (that, of course, was an entirely private affair) but I did work beside him when he was functioning as a crisis manager with patients who were mentally and sometimes physically out of control. He was good; very good.

I remember one patient named Mario. He was a wiry Italian man in his fifties who spoke with a strong accent. Mario was depressed—a gentle man who told me about his disappointments in life while we played cards together in the community room. During his second week on the ward, Mario became suicidal and had to be moved to the isolation room. I was on my coffee break in the staff lounge when one of the nurses rushed in and said that Mario had lost control and they needed me to sit with him until Dr. Ibelle arrived.

The isolation room had no furniture except a mattress on the floor. Mario was cowering in the corner, knees pulled up against his chest, his face a visage of pure terror. He had smeared feces across three of the walls and the smell was overpowering. I glanced around the room in disbelief, then turned back to Mario. His eyes were darting around the room and it was clear that he was hallucinating.

I had known that same terror once as a boy. I had spiked a dangerously high fever and things got extremely weird. I was alone in my room when the windows began to stretch out until they were 15 feet high. The bookcase did the same and I was sure it was about to topple over and bury me in books. My hands felt as though I were clasping a dozen pencils and for some reason, this sensation agitated me to the edge of endurance. When my brother walked by my door, the motion was the visual equivalent of fingernails on a blackboard and I wanted to leap out of the bed, though I barely had the strength to raise my head.

"Get Dad," I moaned, my voice distorted like everything else in the room. More than anything, I wanted my father to arrive. He would know what to do.

So as I sat with Mario, I had some idea of what he was going through. Although I could do nothing to help him, I knew that what he needed most was for me to be calm, reassuring, and project the sense that I had seen this all before.

"Is Doctor Ibelle coming?" he asked.

"Yes, he's on his way."

"*Grazie a Dio*. I hope he gets here soon."

Man, so did I. I'd never seen anything like this. And no matter how calm and reassuring I remained, there wasn't much an 18-year-old freshman on summer break could do for a man who was seeing, hearing, and feeling threatening things that weren't there.

When my father walked into the room, Mario looked up at him with eager eyes. Doctor Ibelle was here—he would know what to do. My father stepped into the room carrying a small stool, set it down, and sat down with an air of relaxed authority.

"Mario, the first thing I need you to do is promise me that you won't try to hurt yourself for the rest of the day. Can you do that?"

"*Si dottore*, I think I can do that."

"Good," he said, then glanced around at the desecrated walls. "So tell me what's going on."

"They told me to do it."

My father didn't have to ask who "they" were.

"The voices," he said.

"They tell me to do terrible things."

"You know these voices are not real."

"I think I know that doctor, but ..." his voice trailed off.

"I know they can be quite threatening," my father said. "But they aren't real and you don't have to do what they say. Do they tell you to hurt yourself?"

"Yes. They say terrible things about me."

"But you know these things are not true."

Mario looked at my father with pleading eyes and shrugged. He was not certain.

"You're a good man, Mario," said my father. "You work hard to support your family and you love your children more than anything in the world. No matter how frightened you get during one of these episodes, you have stay strong—for them. Can you do that?"

"I think so, doctor."

"Good. I'm going to order some medicine that will make the voices and visual hallucinations go away. Billy is going to stay with you until you're feeling better. Then we can come up with a long-term plan."

"*Meno male*," he gasped. "How long will that be, doctor?"

"The nurse will be here with your medicine in less than 15 minutes and it will start taking effect about a half hour after that. So you will be feeling much better in less than an hour."

I could see the tension ease from Mario's shoulders and knew that even though the voices and hallucinations had not receded, my father's calm authority made them less terrifying. I also knew how difficult it was for by father not to react when he walked into that feces-smeared room, and how many horrifying stories he must hear on a daily basis as a therapist. It must have been daunting to be responsible for such damaged lives, but to my father, the weight was irrelevant. As with the war so many years before, it was the business he was in.

CHAPTER 20

Russian Roulette

Just two days after the doctor pulled shrapnel out of Bert's back, he was airborne again. This time the destination was Ruhland, Germany, where they bombed oil refineries. The mission, which lasted 10 hours and covered 1,400 miles, was the longest mission of the war to date for the Fifteenth Air Force.

While on the way to the target, Bert discovered that the ground crew had failed to include his parachute. Rather than report the oversight to the pilot and cause the mission to be aborted, he found a spare parachute with a badly worn harness. This was his first mission since they were nearly shot down over Vienna on March 20, so this discovery must have been particularly unsettling.

> Although I decided to make do with this piece of flotsam, I knew that if the parachute material wasn't rotted away, the condition of the whole pack suggested that if we left the plane together, we would soon part company.

Once again, they encountered heavy flak and fighter attacks, losing six bombers and 61 men. During the bomb run, an angry swarm of German fighters appeared out of the flak smoke. Bert watched them shoot the tail off one bomber and chase another from behind, firing a flurry of cannon shots that caused the bomber to explode.

Maybe it was plane #794 that he saw, which according to army records, was hit by flak, burst into flames, and went into a death spin that killed all 10 crewmen. Or maybe it was #776, which also went down in a spiral

The dual threat of flak and German fighters could make the "Flying Fortress" seem like a balsa wood toy airplane. This one was shot down over Kranenburg, Germany, on April 10, 1945. (US Armed Forces)

of flames as all 10 crew bailed out. One was killed by civilians when he reached the ground while the other nine finished the war as POWs.

Or maybe it was #538, which was hit by both flak and fighter cannons, causing two engines to catch fire, leaving the crew to look on in horror as the flames began to burn the skin off their wings. The pilot, Ralph Bates, entered a steep dive to gain airspeed in hopes of putting out the fires, but when that failed, he gave permission for the crew to bail out. Five airmen bailed and finished the war as POWs, while four others helped Bates regain control of the crippled plane. They finally leveled off at a mere 5,000 feet, and with the wings severely damaged, they limped eastward for an hour and a half, until they crossed the German lines and crash-landed in Poland. All five crewmen survived and eventually made it back to the Sterparone airbase.

During all this chaos, the tail gunner in a nearby plane watched an airman bail out of one of the burning planes. As soon as his parachute opened, it burst into flames and the man plummeted 25,000 feet to his death.

Whichever of these horrors Bert witnessed, he probably didn't have much time to contemplate the fates of fellow airmen—or the sorry state of his rotted parachute—because flak was exploding all around him and he was firing his machine gun furiously at swooping German fighters.

This was also Bert's first encounter with the new German (ME-262) jet fighters, a terrifying innovation they had been warned about for several weeks. In a series of briefings they learned that, while conventional fighters finished an attack by breaking down and away, these new jets were powerful enough to break straight up through the formation, making it impossible for the bombers to shoot at them without hitting their own planes. The new jets rarely made head-on attacks because their closing speed was 500 mph. Combined with the nearly 160 mph cruising speed of the bombers, a head-on attack would mean a closing speed of 660 mph, which was too fast to get off enough shots. So the jets almost always attacked from behind. The only saving grace: the range of the jets was so short that they only had enough time for two attacks before they had to return to base to refuel. Although they had been warned, no briefing could prepare them for the awesome speed and agility of these supercharged planes.

> Lou's voice rang over the intercom: "Here comes one of the bastards now." Then I saw my first Kraut jet break away through our formation after shooting down a bomber. The fellow that Lou spotted came directly in on our tail. Why he didn't fire, I don't know. Perhaps his guns were jammed or he was out of ammunition. In any case, their attack seemed to concentrate on the two boxes [of planes] below us where we could see the skin peel off the bombers before they exploded.

Another narrow escape. Many of the other planes in his group weren't so lucky. This was the second deadliest mission of the entire war for the 483rd Bomb Group.

***

Mention of the 483rd brings up a strange coincidence. As noted, this was the number of my father's bomber group. It was also the address of my mother's childhood home, where she lived throughout the war. So whenever my father wrote to Red, he addressed the envelope to 483 Broadview Terrace, Hartford, Conn. and whenever my mother wrote to Bert, she addressed the envelope to the 483rd Bomb Group.

If my father considered this a positive omen at the time, he never mentioned it. In fact, neither my father nor my mother ever mentioned the uncanny match of these two random numbers.

★★★

With the weather improving, the missions came in rapid succession. Three days after the Ruhland mission, Bert was dropping bombs over Prague, Czechoslovakia. The day before, Bert had a serious sore throat and had been vomiting most of the day, but that didn't stop him from flying the March 25 mission. He was determined to meet his quota as fast as possible so he could go home.

Unlike most of his missions, which were geared towards crippling Nazi fuel supplies and transportation systems, their target this time was the planes themselves. The target was Kbely Airport and Bert's squadron was carrying fragmentation bombs designed to wipe out aircraft and people on the ground.

They were testing the new proximity fuses designed to detonate the bombs 15 feet above the ground. The reason for detonating the bomb before impact was to maximize the destruction of aircraft and troops on the ground. Looking back on this from his retirement, Bert suspected that they were also testing the fuses that would be used to detonate the atomic bombs 1,000 feet above Hiroshima and Nagasaki. It's a chilling thought.

On March 29, Bert was issued a new flight jacket to replace the one torn up by flack on March 20. Now he had new shoes and a new jacket. The medics had changed his bandages several times in the last several days and when they finally came off for good on March 30 he was pleased to report that he had "a couple ugly gashes, but that was all."

April 1, 1945
Boys got the hell knocked out of them again. Two down, several killed and wounded. Target: Maribor, Yugoslavia. Lochansky and Moore shot down. Alerted for flight. Supposed to get Purple Heart tomorrow.

April 2, 1945.
Graz, Austria. Target: marshalling yards. Flak moderate. Fairly easy. Graz is leveled. Entire city burning. Bombs landing everywhere. Alerted again for tomorrow.

April 7, 1945
Only four of Moore's crew alive after crash-landing in Yugoslavia. Chandler killed, Moore's hand shot off. Lochanski's crew killed by Germans in Yugoslavia. Only bombardier and Thomas back.

Bert's crew wasn't activated for the April 1 mission over Maribor, which was a good thing. The plane that was shot down—the one Moore was flying—was the same plane Bert crewed on when they got shot up over Vienna on March 20 and Bert was hit by shrapnel. Army records show that Moore's plane was hit by flak during the bomb run and lost two of its four engines. Several crewmen were injured and Moore called for fighter support to escort them back to Foggia. As they turned for home, the crew began throwing equipment out the bomb bay in a desperate attempt to lighten the plane so they could maintain altitude. They were able to stay with the squadron for 30 minutes before crash-landing near Bosanska Krupa, Yugoslavia. Seven crew members died in the crash. The four survivors avoided capture and eventually made it back to the base to resume the war.

The next day Bert bombed the Graz marshalling yards, but stray bombs leveled the city and set it ablaze. On April 6, they bombed a key railroad bridge at Verona, Italy, so they had now survived 18 missions. They must have wondered how many more times they could spin that barrel and get an empty chamber. Although the odds of survival are 87 percent every time you spin, it sure doesn't feel like that when you get to number 19.

April 8, 1945
Dear Folks: We're over the "hump" now. We've got 18 sorties and 17 to go. We're on the downhill stretch.

★★★

In his retirement-age memoir, my father made no mention of Moore's April 1 crash-landing or Chandler's death. Nor did he say anything about Lochansky's crew being killed by Germans in Yugoslavia. He did not reflect on having bombed the city of Graz into flames. He devoted several pages to describing the various fuses they used on "booby" bombs—fake duds that didn't go off on impact because they were armed with fuses that would detonate when someone—hopefully an enemy soldier, but possibly a woman or child—tried to move them.

The Nazis were the epitome of evil on this earth. They were determined to devour Europe, conquer Russia, and exterminate the Jews. They had to be stopped. But stopping them required the Allies to drop more than 3 million pounds of bombs on and around Vienna, destroying 80,000 buildings and leaving 270,000 people homeless. There is no count of number of civilian deaths.

Bert makes no mention of any of this. As vivid and informative as my father's reflections are, I cannot understand how a person could look back on these experiences and never say anything about the friends and acquaintances killed or the role he was forced to play in the unspeakable carnage of mechanized warfare. But then I've never been through anything even remotely like this, so my inability to understand is both inevitable and irrelevant.

CHAPTER 21

"We Were Tired Beyond Tears"

Less than a week after Bert was hit, Fran's brief rest in the tropics came to an end. He packed his few belongings, took one last look at the crystal stream gurgling beneath the palms, and boarded a ship bound for the next battle of the Pacific War. Before he did all this, he dashed off a quick letter to Bert.

> March 25, 1945
> How's army life in muddy Italy? I know they are keeping you busy as hell flying over Austria. Damn, you birdmen are dropping enough eggs in the Reich homeland.... I have a bit of lousy news from home. Bernyce Jolbert's husband, who I believe was Kenyan, is missing in action. It's pretty dirty to see her get hurt that way. Damn casualties are getting so bad, there are going to be a few more broken-down spirits before the year is up. I hope to Christ it's worth the cost when it's over. But to me it looks like one hell of a big comedy in the Shakespearean sense.
>
> Enough war talk. How's the woman situation? Is that competition giving you much trouble or is the situation well in hand? I have my dough on you Bert.

Fran's destination was Okinawa, where he would take part in Operation *Iceberg*, a massive amphibious assault the size of D-Day. Having already endured an amphibious assault on the Philippines, Fran had a pretty good idea what he was in for. For two months, he had battled the Japanese army on Leyte and now these same fanatical soldiers would be defending their native soil. They would be cornered animals, willing to fight to extinction to defend their homeland.

★★★

April 1, 1945. Easter Sunday. A thunderous barrage of cannon fire erupted from 260 Allied warships, pounding the western beaches of Okinawa where Allied troops were about to land. It was, without a doubt, the strangest landing of the war.

As the iron doors of the landing craft groaned open and the American soldiers poured out into the surf, Fran expected to be mowed down by heavy machine-gun fire like the soldiers on the beaches of Normandy. But he walked ashore with ease, upright and confused by the relative quiet. Once ashore, enemy fire was sporadic and the resistance virtually nonexistent. They expected to fight their way across the dunes on their bellies. But there was no need.

Was this some kind of a trap? Fran kept expecting a surprise attack, but there was none. The battle plan called for three days of heavy fighting to take the main airport, but they walked unmolested onto the runway by noon on the first day. The airport was abandoned.

It was eerie. Where was the enemy?

They encountered only sporadic fighting as they crossed the narrow waist of the island to secure a three-mile belt that stretched from east to west coasts across the island's midsection.

It wasn't until the fourth day, when they turned south towards the capital city of Naha, that all hell broke loose. Over the next 83 days, they endured some of the most vicious fighting of the Pacific war. The three-month hailstorm of cannon fire transformed the lush landscape into a blackened wasteland filled with rotting bodies. It was as if "No-Man's-Land" of the First World War had been transported to the opposite side of the earth. More than 250,000 human lives were extinguished in the battle of Okinawa—including a third of the island's civilian population. The human carnage exceeded the number of deaths caused by the atomic bombs dropped on Hiroshima and Nagasaki combined.

Taking the hill: The sharpshooters of Fran's 96th Division had little cover as they took a series of heavily defended hills. (National Archives, US Signal Corps)

Fran's 96th Infantry Division entered Dante's seventh circle of hell with a nine-day assault on Kakazu Ridge. They began by advancing through heavily mined fields and rice paddies, using tanks for cover as the Japanese gun emplacements on the ridge showered them with bullets and mortar shells. There were mines everywhere. Their world was a massive booby trap. When they finally reached the 280-foot Kakazu Ridge, they were pinned by Japanese fire from above.

In a pre-dawn maneuver, one company fought its way to the top of the west shoulder of the ridge but when they tried to dig in, they realized that the coral ridge was covered by only a few inches of dirt. There was nowhere to hide. The Japanese knew this, of course, and when the American patrol reached the ridge, the Japanese leaped from their defensive positions and sprinted towards the prone Americans firing machine guns and hurling grenades. The charge ended in hand-to-hand combat with bayonets. It was war at its most savage.

The surviving Americans retreated down the hill under the cover of darkness. It took more than a week of heavy fighting to take the Kakazu Ridge, and as soon as they did, they realized that the Japanese had simply retreated to the next ridge, which was equally fortified—and they would have to do it all over again.

★★★

The Japanese had built extensive defensive positions on a series of ridges that gave them an enormous advantage when the Americans arrived. Each ridge was fortified with bunkers, cannons, mortars, machine-gun emplacements, and hundreds of natural caves. These caves and bunkers were connected by 60 miles of tunnels so that the entire Japanese force on Okinawa could be underground where they would be protected from the furious assault of Allied gunships and aircraft. The tunnels made it possible for the Japanese to move soldiers and armaments around the battlefield without any exposure to enemy fire. They could simply duck down into the tunnels and pop up in a completely different position, sometimes behind the American lines of assault. They often did this at night, so their sleep was fitful at best, a few stolen moments during lulls in the fighting.

When they were finally overpowered by the Americans, they simply moved back to the next line of defense, also on a high ridge. As a result, the Japanese always occupied the high ground and the Americans were forever sprinting across unprotected open fields, then battling uphill against an enemy that was entirely dug in. To make matters worse, the valleys were both tight and steep, which meant that whenever the Americans launched an assault on one hill, the Japanese had clear shots at them from other nearby hills. The American troops were perpetually in a crossfire. It was like diving headfirst into a woodchipper.

★★★

As soon as they captured Kakazu Ridge, the battered and depleted 96th marched deeper into hell to assault Hacksaw Ridge. Exhausted

Soldiers from Fran's 96th Division worked in tandem with flame-throwing tanks to attack the Japanese cave system. (US National Archives)

soldiers crept through fields littered with spent shell casings, discarded ammunition boxes, disabled vehicles, and decomposing bodies. By now it was mid-April and they had been fighting non-stop for two weeks.

During those two weeks, American ships landed a new weapon on the island—flame-throwing tanks designed to blowtorch the landscape. As a tank lumbered up the hills, it would pull up close to one of the enemy caves and belch its dragon's breath into the hole, burning everything and everyone inside. The stench of burned flesh filled the humid air. It was inescapable, clinging to the nostrils and completing the vision of the Hell that mankind had so deftly created on the green surface of our earth.

For six days, the 96th fought to a stalemate on Hacksaw Ridge then, in what must have seemed like a miracle, they were relieved by fresh soldiers and granted 10 days of rest. They trudged through the carnage to a camp that was set in an unscarred region north of the fighting.

Soon after he arrived, Fran dashed off a V-mail to Bert:

> April 13, 1945
> Dear Bert:
> Here I be on beautiful Okinawa for my second taste of combat and another star on my Asia Pacific ribbon. The fight is rougher than I experienced in the Philippines, but with God's help, I've come through without a scratch so far. At present, we are in the rear taking a rest after running those bastards out of hills for a couple weeks. They are dug in like a bunch of rats and they threw every damn thing at us before we dug them out. I'm also getting a taste of their artillery and though they haven't a great number of [censored] they still put a little lead in our asses now and then. The island is really a wonderful spot. Days are similar to southern California, sunny and dry. Nights are chilly and we love our GI blankets. So in all Bert, everything is working out well and I hope the same goes for you over there. Maybe it will be over by the time this letter reaches you. It would be great if your outfit was transferred to this island. We could rain hell. Oh yes, I put another notch in the BAR. Got him on the first night. I also have claim to a couple of possibles. Have you heard from Bob? He must be well into Germany by now.

I can't help but wonder how much the presence of Army censors influenced the content of Fran's V-mail. How could he emerge from all this and write an upbeat note about the beauty of the island? When I first read this V-mail I didn't know anything about what Fran had been through, but as I researched the movements of the 96th, the tone seemed odd given the unbridled terror of the previous three weeks. The 96th had suffered so many casualties in the previous two weeks that they received 2,600 replacements to fill their depleted ranks.

I think a clue to Fran's state of mind can be found in the post-war writings of another member of the 96th, an artist by the name of Carl Albin Hall. In his post-war memoir, *The Broken Urn*, he describes the fighting: Here are a few short excerpts:

"Tired beyond tears": Members of the 96th collapse in exhaustion during a brief lull in the fighting. (US Armed Forces, National Archives)

> Lucifer walked the ridges, the escarpments, the rice fields....Dismembered bodies became testaments of struggle and sorrow. Human idiocy surrounded us on all sides.
>
> War assumed more importance than rest, or food, or comfort or companionship, becoming the only coherent tie we had with life. [I] had given up the close bonds of friendship because friends were eternally lost and replacements came and left too fast.
>
> We were tired beyond tears.*

It's likely that Fran shared the same rest camp with Hall since they were in the same regiment. I have no idea whether they knew one another. While perched on a bucolic hill overlooking the village of Koza, Hall describes the village below, which was untouched by flamethrowers

* Carl Albin Hall, *The Broken Urn*: published in connection with an exhibition entitled "Carl Hall: World War II Drawings" presented at the Hallie Ford Museum of Art at Willamette University, 2004, pp. 6, 8, 46.

or mortar fire. The serenity of his perch must have been profoundly disorienting, given the mechanized slaughter he participated in during the two weeks before. I suspect that Hall's decision to write about himself in the third person is a measure of the level of trauma he suffered:

> Memory gnawed on all this, trying to find some life-giving sustenance, some form of sanity where he would be found again to be human and unafraid. He needed to find some budding humanity outside himself vast enough to hold all his woe, all of this constant human degradation.

They were so desperate to touch life again. They yearned for contact with some fragment of the world that was untainted by the inferno raging less than a mile away and wanted to remember what it was like to feel human. Hall sat stunned beneath his tree—yes, a living tree—momentarily content as he watched the sun ease itself down into the East China Sea.

> The evening fires flickered in the thatched huts; he heard talking in the darkness, the bubble of children's laughter well up over the barking dogs and the far-off sound of a stringed instrument twanging in the evening like some reawakened heartbeat.... It was like being reborn after wallowing in all the suffering of hell.

Maybe this is why so many soldiers refuse to reflect on their time in the war—a time when they had to play a role in Satan's game, sometimes taking the role of Satan himself. So they build a wall around this portion of their lives, vowing to never peek over the top of that wall.

Funny stories ... sure.

Facts ... maybe.

How they felt ... never.

CHAPTER 22

A Narrow Escape

Back at the Sterparone air base, the weather was steadily improving and by mid-April, they were battling oppressive heat. The sudden change in climate created an odd phenomenon in which they were blasted by the dust blowing off a crust of dried dirt, even as their boots broke through that same crust and sank ankle-deep into the mush below.

On one of his April missions, Bert sustained another injury, but this time it had nothing to do with enemy fire. As already noted, air expands dramatically when flying above 25,000 feet. In one of his letters home the year before, he had described how his instructor dramatized this fact by tying off an unused condom and placing it in the altitude simulator. It expanded to the size of an eggplant, then exploded.

During a mission in April 1945, this same phenomenon caused a tiny pocket of air below one of Bert's fillings to expand and pop the filling out of his tooth. The resulting crater became inflamed, which gave him an opportunity to experience field dentistry in its most literal sense.

> The good doctor took me out into the fields where he had set up his equipment—a straight chair, a table with instruments, and a foot pedal drill. When I sat down in the execution chair he did not say "Hang on" but I got the message in short order. He began pedaling furiously; the drill bore into my tooth (all the way to my big toe?) The sweat poured off his brow; the smoke out of my mouth. In a panicky voice he kept shouting, "I can't stop. I'll get stuck." I probably should have felt some degree of sympathy for the poor man in his hour of distress but I was much too busy creating new curses for his ancestors.

A few days after surviving his encounter with the field dentist, Bert learned the fate of one of the guys who crash-landed in Yugoslavia earlier in the month. Although seven of his crewmates died in the crash, Bert wrote that this fellow was rescued by local partisans who stashed him in a barbershop, then led him out the back door, hid him in a hay wagon, and drove him out of town before handing him over to Allied forces. He heard of another airman who was shot down over southern Austria swiped some old peasant clothes, stole a cow, and walked across the country to safety as if he were a farmer bringing his cow to market.

★★★

Between missions, the crew struggled to find ways to stave off boredom. One option was to make the 20-mile trip to Foggia in one of the army trucks that made daily runs to the city. These trucks were usually packed with airmen, often so packed that there was standing room only or even less.

> I once rode the twenty-plus miles sitting on the right front fender, holding onto the headlight grill. On another occasion, I rode on the outside of the rack body with my feet splayed, standing on about one inch of metal outside the rack. Two fellows on the inside held me against the rack by grasping my belt. I helped by keeping a vice-grip on one of the side boards. Turns away from my side of the truck were particularly difficult since, while the truck turned away from me, my body had an unnerving impulse to keep going straight ahead, thus confirming the lessons learned in high school physics.

On one occasion, Bert missed the last truck back to base. It was a moonless night and he walked to the edge of town "feeling rather lonely and forlorn" with a dim hope of hitchhiking 15 miles back to the base. He stood there, thumb out, on a dark road in a foreign country that just a few months before, had been our enemy in the war. It seemed an impossible and slightly dangerous task. To his surprise, a truck eventually stopped and offered him a ride as far as Lucera, a town six miles south of the air base at Sterparone. Bert hopped in and was relieved to have a ride for the first 10 miles of his journey back to the base. When they arrived in Lucera, the driver left him off just outside the gate of the walled city. As Bert watched the truck drive through the gate into town, its headlights flashed on a group of figures coming Bert's way.

> I was immediately on guard and it wasn't long before my suspicions were confirmed. A stone landed near me and then another. I could hear them closing in around me. We could not see each other but I could approximately locate them by the sounds they made. I kept moving as quietly as I could, hoping to eventually escape down the road to Sterparone. They had just about closed the trap around me when a truck came around the corner, caught the scene in his headlights and slowed just enough for me to roll onto the tailgate and we sped off down the hill under hail of rocks. There were a few dents in the truck but no injuries.

It was another reminder that there are many ways to get seriously injured during a war that have little to do with combat. Bert had no idea who his attackers were or why they were hurling rocks at him. It could have been because of his uniform, since it had been less than a year since the Allies invaded southern Italy. The Germans still controlled the northern portion of the country and it would be another month before Mussolini was captured and executed by Italian resistance fighters. Ordinary citizens in Italy were very much divided as to which side they favored in the war.

But if you think about it, what are the chances that a band of Fascist sympathizers would lay in wait for a stray GI to walk into a remote Italian town. And what are the chances they would be armed only with rocks? So the more likely explanation is that they were just a band of roving young men who were impoverished and angered by the ravages of war. Southeastern Italy was poor before the war, but since the invasion, many citizens lived among the ruins. So when a uniformed GI showed up hitchhiking on a cold April night, it was as if a pack of hungry dogs had come across an unsuspecting deer.

Bert narrowly escaped his attackers because another truck driver saw what was about to happen and slowed so he could jump into the back. The driver dropped him off a mile down the road and Bert walked the rest of the way back to the base unharmed.

In the days that followed, Bert's morale began to falter. A sense of frustration and despair began to leak into his just-the-facts diary entries.

April 8, 1945
Briefed for guard duty tonight.... We're suckers for flying in this theater. They're treating us like dogs.

In his retirement-age reflections, Bert describes the multiple sources of his squadron's plummeting morale: 1) unsanitary food that led to bouts of diarrhea at 25,000 feet; 2) combat crews pulling guard duty, often on the night before a mission, and 3) resentment about the constant press coverage and fawning Army publicity about the Eighth Air Force in England. While bomber crews in England were heroically referred to as "The Mighty Eighth," their peers in Italy became known as "The Forgotten Fifteenth."

> We felt slighted when we constantly heard radio reports about the exploits of the Eighth Air Force and heard reports of DFCs [the Distinguished Flying Cross] and other awards being handed out by the barrelful while we couldn't get deserved awards for many of our personnel.

April 9, 1945
Guard duty 2–6 a.m. Missed a top-secret mission to the front because of guard. Playing tin soldier is more important than flying. 99th bombed British troops. God, what a bunch of muddle-heads in this Air Force.

April 10, 1945
Missed another mission to the front today because we weren't on the battle order yesterday. God, are we disgusted!

April 16, 1945
Roped in on J's court-martial as a witness. Scratched from mission.

In spite of his plummeting morale, Bert maintained an optimistic face in his letters home. There was no need to worry his parents about the danger and frustration he lived with every day. Besides, any complaints would never get past the Army censors.

> April 23, 1945
> Dear Folks:
> Well it was this time two years ago that I was sworn into the Army. I sure have seen a lot and done a lot since then. I hope it is less time than that when we're all finally given those little old white discharge papers. What a day that will be! No point in looking that far ahead though. The main thing is to get this part of it over with first. I've got 21 in now, only 14 more to go.

Like all airmen, Bert kept a tally of his missions, dreaming of the day he would reach his quota and earn a one-way ticket home. Each time he missed a mission—whether it was because of guard duty, a bum tooth, or being called as a witness in a bogus court-martial trial—his long-awaited flight back across the Atlantic was delayed. He was particularly incensed by having to testify in J's trial because he had already told the prosecutors he had not seen the defendant on the night the man was supposedly drunk on guard duty. He had nothing to add to the prosecution and made this infinitely clear, so he was furious that he had to miss another mission in order to take the stand and say he saw nothing. Bert's sour spirits may have been calmed a bit by a letter he received from Mary Jane.

> April 15, 1945
> Golly but I have been thinking a lot about you today.... Yesterday I went out for my first driving lesson with my father. I bet I can make a car jerk more than anyone else can. My pop has hope for me anyway. If you were home, I'd ask you to teach me. Oh, you poor guy.... Gosh do I miss hearing from you. It seems like months since I received the last letter. I hope it's the mail service that's to blame and that you are okay.

In her letters, Mary Jane often mentioned the songs playing on the radio as she wrote, and the tunes she chose to mention must have lifted Bert's spirits—"Dream of You," "A Little on the Lonely Side," "Make Believe." One passage in particular struck me as ironic, knowing now what Mary Jane couldn't have known at the time.

> April 15, 1945
> … Bing Crosby is singing now. He's the best. I was looking at a movie magazine yesterday and was sadly disappointed to learn that he is bald.

Guess what mom—you're going to marry Bert and you are going to remain happily married for 62 years. But he's going to go bald just like Bing. On the holidays, my father liked to croon "White Christmas" along with Bing while we decorated the tree. He wasn't bad.

CHAPTER 23

April 1945: The Final Fury

In early April the Fifteenth Air Force shifted its focus from northern Europe to the Po Valley in northern Italy, where Allied forces were mounting a major land offensive to pin the German army against the Alps. It was the culmination of a bloody campaign that began in September 1943 with the Allied invasion of Italy near Naples and continued for a year and a half as the Allied armies battled their way to Rome and across the Apennines. With Allied forces sweeping eastward across northern Europe and Russian forces slogging westward across Poland and Romania, the goal was to mount a major offensive from the south to squeeze the Nazis like a pimple on the face of civilization.

The job of the 483rd Airborne was to: 1) bomb the front lines of German troops in the Po Valley north of Bologna to soften them up for the invasion, and 2) cut off German supply lines through the Brenner Pass, which runs through the Alps from Verona to Innsbruck.

On an April 6 mission to bomb a key railroad bridge in Verona, Ben became violently ill at 29,000 feet. This presented a major problem, since he needed to remain on oxygen to stay alive and had no one to help him in his tiny tail gunner compartment.

> This required him to crawl up to the waist where Gene and I could tend to him. We had to remove his oxygen mask each time he vomited and replace it as soon as he stopped. In addition, we had to alternately plug him in to our oxygen systems. This had to be done at least every minute since none of us could stay effective or even conscious if deprived of oxygen for much longer. This process kept up until we got down to 20,000 feet.

On April 17, while returning from a mission to bomb German troops near Bologna, Bert witnessed an all-out artillery attack by the Allied ground forces against the Germans. "I would not have wanted to be on that tiny plot of ground," he wrote in his retirement-age reflections. The next day, he returned to the Po Valley to bomb the same area again, an operation that was repeated twice a day until the German's retreated.

> The constant saturation bombing of a small area with double missions day after day must have been horrific for those on the ground. I once tried to roughly calculate the scope of destruction. I figured that there had to be at least one bomb for every three square feet.

Two days later, their mission was to sever German supply lines in the Brenner Pass.

> **April 20, 1945**
> Woke us at 4 a.m. and told us to fly with Foster. Flack intense, heavy, accurate. Ship from 301st nose and #4 engine blown off. 2 chutes. P-51 in flames—pilot out. 840th lost two. I feel more beat and aching after this one than any other. Ears aching and plugged.

This mission had its own unique set of terrors. The Brenner Pass was so narrow and the Alps so high, they were forced to "dive-bomb" the rail lines and bridges, losing 10,000 feet in a matter of minutes.

> The dive to the target was necessitated by the complexity of the bomb pattern. Because the Brenner Pass is so narrow, the Air Force had groups of coming into the drop area from different angles and at different altitudes. Their arrival over the target had to be precisely timed. Nothing ever goes as planned, so some formations were dropping their loads through other formations. Since there was a group directly above us that was about to release, we had to get out of the way in a hurry.

The result of this airborne roller coaster—one without tracks or seat belts—was that Bert developed a painful case of aortitis, an inner ear inflammation that rendered him deaf for several days. He missed two more missions because of the malady.

★★★

In their quest to make up lost missions, Bert and Ben, the tail gunner, lobbied heavily to fly with Joe Nolan, who had been three years ahead of Bert at Bulkeley High School in Hartford. Nolan had been a popular student and was now a highly respected pilot, so my father was eager to fly with someone he knew and respected. Nolan was going to be the co-pilot on my father's favorite plane, #327, a well-maintained bomber that he had flown on during seven missions already, including his first mission on Christmas day.

A friend of theirs was in charge of scheduling, so Bert and Ben assumed they were shoo-ins for the extra mission. But for some unexplained reason, Bert's friend refused their request. "You don't want to go," he said, dismissing them without further explanation. When they begged him to reconsider, he responded with a simple, "You're NOT going."

In his retirement-age reflections, Bert wondered why his buddy refused to let him fly that day. He doubted his friend had any kind of premonition, but given what happened, it was hard not to wonder. Whatever the reason, the events of the next day confirm that Bert's buddy was right when he insisted, "You don't want to go."

> **April 25, 1945**
> Boys got hell at Linz. Lost three ships. One boy knocked right out of the tail. Multi down and killed. Joe Nolan down again on his 35th mission … Alerted for mission tomorrow. Scared as hell.

Those last three words jumped out at me: "Scared as hell."

It was the only time in either his wartime journal or his retirement-age memoirs that he ever mentioned fear. It had been Nolan's 35th mission. Had he returned, he would have been eligible for discharge. After 23 missions, Bert must have felt like his number was due to come up soon. He had spun the barrel 23 times and so far the chamber had been empty every time. Would number 24 be the time that his high-altitude Russian roulette ended with a bullet in the chamber? Nolan's fate had him seriously spooked.

Army records include several eye-witness accounts of the crash by airmen in nearby planes. These reports indicate that #327 was hit by flak four times at 27,000 feet causing the left wing to stream flames. Witnesses saw six parachutes as the plane flew for Russia, lost control, spun towards the ground, and exploded in midair over Linz, Austria. Two men died in the explosion, one died when his parachute failed to open and a fourth died when he was shot and killed by angry civilians as his parachute neared the ground. This was Nolan. The remaining six airmen were captured by an angry mob that turned them over to the SS. They finished the war as POWs at the Mauthausen concentration camp, where they witnessed the desecration of Nolan's body by German SS soldiers. His remains were never found.

I will have to jump ahead in the story for a moment because Nolan's fate remained uncertain for a month. Several men were seen parachuting out of the plane before it exploded, but it wasn't clear whether Nolan was among them. By the time Bert got the news, the war in Europe was over and he was waiting to be reassigned to the Pacific.

> **May 25, 1945**
> Found out that Joe Nolan was killed in his 'chute close to the ground. Sinton [the pilot], navigator and engineer went down with ship. Two waist gunners, Zinn and Campbell, got out. Radioman also killed.

A few weeks later, Bert was on furlough in Hartford, awaiting his next assignment. It is the only time in his retirement-era reflections that he comments on the death of a fellow airman:

> Knowing the fate of Nolan presented me with some problems when I got home. People there knew that we were in the same squadron and kept asking about him. Since the family had not been notified of his death, I had to evade people and avoid questions. Some of the more astute ones recognized the situation and backed off. The death notice didn't come for about two months after the war was over.

I don't know anything about Joe Nolan and never heard my father mention his name. But after poking around the internet for a while, I was able to find a copy of the 1938 Bulkeley High School yearbook. It describes him as a popular student with "an electric personality" who was destined for success.

JOSEPH FRANCIS NOLAN
"Joe"

"Nothing succeeds so well as success."

A. A. 1, 2, 3, 4; Boys' Club 1, 3, 4; Art Club 4, President 4; Student Council 1, 3, 4; Legislative Club 3, 4; Mathematics Club 4; Junior Dramatic Club 1, 2; Torch Business Board 1, 2; Junior Usher. Washington Street School. Trinity College.

Besides having an amazing amount of dynamic energy which he used in his position as Business Manager of the Dial, Joe had an electric personality which attracted everyone to him. These talents are likely to help him forge ahead in the future.

Joe Nolan's photo from his high school yearbook. (Bulkeley High School)

But instead, he's just another name on a WWII plaque somewhere, largely forgotten over the decades because he never had a chance to make his mark on the world or have a family of his own to keep his memory alive.

★★★

Let's return now to April 26, 1945. The war in Europe is still raging at full throttle. For Bert, it is the day of Mission #24. This was a particularly nerve-wracking mission because the next day the entire crew was scheduled to begin their first leave, which was to take place on the island of Capri. This made them especially nervous. After all, no one wants to be blown out of the sky on the day before vacation.

The target that day was an ammunition dump in Bolzano, Italy, in the southern Alps leading up to the Brenner Pass. The Fifth Army had finally broken through the German defenses in the Po Valley and were fanning out across northern Italy. In his war diary, my father noted the number of antiaircraft guns (118), the temperature, (44 below zero), and the altitude (27,000 feet). But it was a rather cryptic notation that caught the attention of my sharp-eyed brother when he came across my father's war diary in the basement one summer when we were kids. The direct quotation my father attributes to us in the following passage is highly implausible, but the overall spirit of the interaction is accurate.

> Many years later, my two teenage boys found my diary. They eventually came to me and said, "Dad, we've been studying this thing for days and we've figured out all your shorthand and symbols except for this one: What does CIP mean?" I hemmed and hawed for a moment and then fessed up. It means "Crapped In Pants."

Of course we thought this was hilarious and demanded an explanation. My father explained that the night before the mission, dinner produced some rather alarming symptoms among the airmen scheduled to fly the next morning. Many were grounded, but my father, blessed with his iron stomach, wasn't bothered by the tainted food—or so he thought. When he noticed his stomach gurgling over northern Italy, he became worried about Ben, who was by himself in the tail gunner's position and had food-induced vomiting on a previous mission.

> Just before we turned on the bomb run, I had a mighty urge to break wind and while that bit of behavior was in process, I called to Ben and said, "Ben, how is ... is ... Oh no!" As we started to lose altitude after the bomb run, I began the arduous task of stripping down until I was wearing nothing but my oxygen mask, goggles, and helmet. I cleaned up, and since it was 44 below zero, I did not waste any time when getting dressed again. As we passed over Bologna, I dumped my summer underwear into the city.

My father's final hostile act of the war is the stuff of family legend.

★★★

The day after Bert dumped his payload on Bologna, bad weather forced the Air Corps to cancel the crew's flight to Capri. Unwilling to miss an opportunity to see more of the country, Frank insisted that they hitchhike. Their second ride took them across the mountains that run down the spine of Italy.

> The trip across the mountains in a British lorry was an experience. Italians drive on the right side of the road as we do. The lorry was a right-hand drive. When attempting to pass on the narrow, winding mountain roads, we had to pull all the way to the left shoulder before the driver could see if the road ahead was clear. Standing in the back of the truck, we could often see potential disaster hurling in our direction as the driver swung out for a look-see. On a number of occasions, we banged on the cab roof to warn him to turn back in.

They spent their first night on leave in Naples where they went out on the town to celebrate and finished the night singing drunkenly on Via Roma with a group of British soldiers and locals.

> The sense of freedom on arriving in Naples was wonderful. After spending months in cold, wet, muck and dust—living six or more to the tent—the prospect of living like humans again provoked an almost overwhelming sense of well-being. Standing on a corner of a major thoroughfare in a foreign land, singing songs with strangers from other countries and cultures just felt GOOOD!

The next day, they caught a steamer to paradise—the island of Capri. The weather was perfect, the island beautiful, and the accommodations luxurious. They stayed at the Morgano Tiberio, a five-star hotel that was paid for by the US Armed Forces. It was a marvel. Bert described the luxury in a letter to his favorite aunt and uncle.

> May 1945
> It's one of those really high-class hotels used for European tourists before the war. The beds had box springs, with innerspring mattresses on top of that. They were so comfortable that we couldn't sleep well in them at first. We also had a bathtub with hot water. Just sit and soak. That was the first time I felt clean in six months ... The meals were something else again. Waiters in tuxedos, dinner music, tablecloths and the meals were served in about 5 courses. We ate like kings.

For the next eight days, they savored the beauty of Capri, visiting Tiberius's Palace (Villa Jovis), the Blue Grotto, and Anacapri. One afternoon, they bribed the funicular operator to let them drive the car up and down the mountainside for 45 minutes between his regularly scheduled runs.

On May 5, they bummed a ride back to the mainland on a PT boat, making the two-and-a-half-hour crossing in just 45 minutes. Two days after they arrived back at the base in Sterparone, news broke that the war in Europe was over. Mary Jane immediately dashed off a letter.

> May 7, 1945
> Germany surrenders! I can just imagine how happy the fellows are over there. Oh, the celebrating that must be going on—Oh boy! I should feel excited but I'm afraid I'm not. There is still Japan. At any rate, half of it is over and I pray the rest won't take too long.

At Sterparone, the celebrating was almost as dangerous as the war. Ecstatic airmen fired guns and lobbed flares among the closely packed tents. Bert spent most of the night putting out grass fires that threatened to burn down the tents and detonate 55-gallon barrels of aviation fuel that stood beside each tent to feed the makeshift stoves.

> Sometime during the night, someone sprayed our latrine area with a machine gun. Fortunately, no one was busy in there at the time. I was relieved when morning came and things settled down.

> May 8, 1945
> Dear Mary Jane:
> There's no use trying to explain how we feel because you must feel the same and know that the feeling can't be put into words. It's wonderful to know that we are safe now—for a while at least, and that this part of the war is *finite*. The celebrating back in the States must have been something to witness. I wish I could have been there.

For the first time in more than two years of mortal danger, they were able to relax.

> May 12, 1945
> Dear Aunt June and Uncle Ben:
> Boy am I glad it's over. They were getting a little too close to little old Ibelle. Those squareheads sure can handle a flak gun. I was able to get in 24 missions before they gave up. We bombed Germany, Austria, Italy and Hungary. Vienna was the toughest by far. That's where I got my Purple Heart. I could never understand how we got across that town as many times as we did.... Those German jet planes are really fast. One Kraut broke away right through our box doing better than 500 mph with its power off!!... Well, it's over for us for a while now anyway. We'll be going back to the States for further training before we have to go to the Pacific. We don't know how long it will be before we go back.

CHAPTER 24

Dear Mom Ibelle

While Bert waited in Italy for his next assignment, the war in the Pacific raged on. Two days after Germany surrendered, the Bert/Fran seesaw shifted again as Fran's rest break on Okinawa ended and the 96th returned to battle. Before he left, he wrote a letter to my grandmother thanking her for the pictures she sent and congratulating them on their move to a single-family home, where they would no longer have to deal with their cranky landlord.

> April 20, 1945
> Dear Mom Ibelle:
> ... Right now I'm planted on Japanese soil. The place is Okinawa Jima. I must admit, it's quite a beautiful island and is a far cry from the muddy, tropical Philippines. The days here would remind you of southern California, being dry, sunny, and at moderate temperature ... So all in all, I'm fine and everything is going along as best as possible. I'm still sweating out the day when we all can get together again and enjoy those great informal visits again. Give my regards to Howard and June [Bert's father and younger sister].
> Love Fran

Despite the upbeat tone of the letter, there was nothing cheery about Fran's return to the front. As they trudged through the carnage, they passed trucks coming in the opposite direction carrying the bodies of dead soldiers stacked like cordwood. The holes created by artillery shells had filled with rainwater and maggots covered the swollen bodies of the dead.

Their objective was yet another line of Japanese defenses along a series of hills named King, Love, Easy, Fox, and Pinnacle. Their ultimate goal was to capture a pyramid-shaped outcropping known as Conical Hill. This was the main observation center for the Japanese and as such, the key to firing their artillery and mortars with such unnerving accuracy.

The battle for Conical Hill would be the worst fighting of the 83-day battle of Okinawa. American soldiers followed the flame-throwing tanks across the flatlands to protect them from the increasing numbers of Japanese schoolboys, the *Tekketsu Kinnōtai* ("Student Units of Blood and Iron for Emperor"), who had been trained as suicide bombers, running up to the tanks with explosive they would toss under the wheels or down the hatch.

When tanks couldn't reach a Japanese cave because of the terrain, troops fought their way up the hills, often in hand-to-hand combat with bayonets and knives. They approached the caves by wheeling tanks of fuel and 300 feet of hose to pump a mixture of gasoline and napalm into the caves, then backed away and ignited the mixture by hurling phosphorous grenades into the hole. This produced an earth-shaking explosion and a few moments later, isolated columns of smoke poured from caves hundreds of yards in every direction, providing vivid evidence of the interconnected tunnels system the Japanese used to move troops and engineer their escape.

The *Tekketsu Kinnōtai* were child soldiers enlisted by the Japanese Army to carry out suicide missions, like running up to American tanks carrying bombs. (US National Archives)

There is nothing to indicate that Fran participated in flame-throwing teams, but he certainly saw and smelled the results.

For the next two weeks, they fought an uphill battle against an enemy that popped up and disappeared like marmots all over the adjoining hills. The rain ensured another level of misery. They were constantly wet, muddy, and had no change of clothing. Lice and fleas were everywhere. The rain washed maggots off the corpses and into the mud. Since fires would give away their position, they had no hot food or coffee. The landscape had been devastated by flamethrowers and artillery fire, so there wasn't a tree or bush for miles.

In the midst of this fighting, my grandmother sent a letter to Fran:

> May 16, 1945
> Dear Fran:
>
> We were so glad to get your letter. How do you find time to write when there is so much going on there? Now that VE Day is here, we will be able to concentrate everything on the Pacific. It may bring you home sooner. We certainly hope so. The rumor is that all B-17s will come home to Bradley Field [in Hartford] and the boys redeployed from there. We are hoping that Bert will come in there soon before being sent to the Pacific.... Have you heard from Bert since he was wounded? He claims it was not serious.... Very little mail is coming in from Europe. All space is taken up with returning soldiers. That is as it should be.... Bob Pabuda is in the hospital with yellow jaundice. He expects to be hospitalized for some time. He is somewhere in Germany. Rest and proper diet will clear that up. Well Fran, I'd like to write you a long interesting letter but as I said before, I cannot seem to collect any news. Is there anything I can send you? This letter leaves us all in good health. Hope you are well too.
>
> Loads of love.
> Mom Ibelle

★★★

It took me a moment to realize that there was something very strange about this letter. Why did my father have a letter that his mother sent to Fran? When I slid the letter back into its envelope I found the answer. Each letter sent by a soldier had to be reviewed by an Army censor. The sensor blotted out any sensitive information, then gave his approval by writing his name and the date in a circle just below the mailing address. I glanced at the censor's circle and there it was ... a single word: Deceased.

My father had that letter because it was returned to my grandmother unopened. She must have put it in the box where she saved all my father's letters home. My grandmother had posted her letter to Fran on May 16 and by the time it arrived in Okinawa, Fran was already dead. Now I understood why I'd never heard of him. Unlike Bob and Saul, he never made it back. He died in the last battle of the war when he was within spitting distance of the future he would never have.

In a letter Fran sent a month before, he had written to my grandmother about how he and Bob were about to turn 21. He never made it. Nor did he make it to the long-awaited reunion of the old gang in Hartford. He never married the gorgeous Ruth from the University of Kentucky. He never had kids to carry his memory. He was just another stone thrown into the lake, its ripples disappearing before they reached the shore. Gone. Poof. Like he never happened. A dozen passages from his letters raced through my head:

> "Darn, I never thought I could go gaga for a girl at my present age, but love's a screwy thing, it hits you like a rocket."

> "What's the matter, is your right arm (or should I say hand) preoccupied that much? Hands off Oscar and dash me off a letter."

> "After all that training all the bastards can find for us is getting dumped into the infantry. So shoo shoo baby, off to become a Jap hunter. That's my position now: screwed, blewed, and tattooed."

> "No kidding, if she had come home with me, I believe we would have gotten married. No use moaning. There are still plenty of years ahead."

> "Dear Mom Ibelle: Bob and I will be 21 come May. Turning into young men aren't we? Won't be long when we plan to start homes."

> "Damn casualties are getting so bad, there are going to be few more broken-down spirits before the year is up. I hope to Christ this is worth the cost when this is over. But to me it looks like one hell of a big comedy in the Shakespearean sense."

Fran on the beach in 1942, the summer before he went to war. (The Ibelle family)

Francis A. Brighenti was killed three days before his 21st birthday while clearing out an enemy cave. That night, several hours after Fran died, the annual monsoons let loose a deluge of historic proportions. It was as if nature were trying to scrub the bloodied land clean. But soldiers on both sides just waited for the worst of the torrent to pass, then resumed their punch-drunk slugfest for another month.

★★★

Although I never met him, I developed a strong attachment to Fran while reading his letters to my father. I was shaken when I stumbled upon his fate, and desperately wanted to know what happened. There was nothing on the internet. Obituaries from that long ago have not been digitized, and it was hardly news that another soldier had been killed in World War II.

I tried to track down my father's friends from his Bulkeley High days, but all I found was obituary after obituary, dead ends in the most literal sense. I had waited too long.

I searched for other Brighentis in Connecticut, but none of them were the right line of the family. Why couldn't I find the names of anyone from his immediate family?

I got the answer from the 1940 census. Francis Brighenti of Ward 15, Hartford, Connecticut, was a 15-year-old boy at the time. He had three sisters, which explained the absence of surviving relatives with the Brighenti name. How could I find his sisters if I didn't even know their last names? I stuck with it, unwilling to accept defeat, and finally turned up an obituary for a Louise B. Quinn whose parents were named Brighenti and who was predeceased by a brother named Francis. I went back to the 1940 census and, sure enough, Fran had a sister named Louise. So I set out to find Louise only to learn that she had died at age 100 just three months before my search.

I soon found a second obituary for an Elise Grant, who also had parents named Brighenti and a dead brother named Francis. She had died at age 93 in 2019. But unlike Louise, sister #2 had some surviving children—Wayne and Pamela. It was a wild shot, but I decided to give it a try. I searched the internet for all the Wayne Grants in Connecticut. There are a lot of them and no one got back to me. So I decided to take an even longer shot and searched for Pamela Grant. The likelihood that she was still using her maiden name seemed slim. But then—Bingo!—I found a Pamela Grant LLC in Middletown, Connecticut, and the owner of record had graduated from Bulkeley High School in Hartford.

I was thrilled when I received a return email from Pam with her phone number. But when I called her the next day, she didn't know much about her uncle, other than he died on Okinawa during WWII. After all, he was dead long before she was born. She sent me his obituary, but that only provided the date of his death; no information about how it happened.

Pam suggested that I try talking with "Auntie," who was 90 years old at the time. Fran's youngest sister, Dorothy, was 13 years old when her brother was killed. She was 11 years old when she last saw him while he was on furlough just before going overseas.

It was another long shot, but I gave her a call.

"Who is this, again?"

"My name is Bill Ibelle. I'm the son of Bert Ibelle who was a friend of your brother."

"Bert Ibelle?"

"Yes, Bert."

Pause.

"My gosh, I was just thinking about Bert the other day. He became a doctor at Hartford Hospital, didn't he?"

"Yes, a psychologist."

"Well good for him. You say you're his son?"

"Yes, I'm writing about his experience in World War II and …."

"They were like brothers. Bert was over the house all the time. I was just a little girl at the time but I remember your father well. When they went off to college, Bert sent me a football banner from Dartmouth. I had it on my wall the whole time I was growing up."

I was starting to tear up, although I don't know why.

"My brother was very tall—and very handsome. The last time he was home from the Army—it was just before he went overseas—your father came over with Bob Pabuda and they performed one of their skits for my parents. He came over that night with Mary Jane. Did he ever end up marrying her?"

"Yes. Mary Jane is my mother."

"Then you are a very lucky young man."

"I don't know about 'young,' but yes, I'm very lucky."

"Bert and Mary Jane drove Fran to the train that night. That was the last time I saw him."

If my father and mother drove Fran to the train—that means they were the last friends or family to see him alive.

I can envision the scene: the train station at night; the warm summer air; my teenage father and mother on a date as they shake the hand of a close friend leaving for the war. The train pulls away with a hiss and the screech of iron wheels, then they are left on the platform … in the silence … with

Bert and Fran (right) with Fran's mother while on leave before being deployed. This was the last time his family or hometown friends saw Fran alive. (The Ibelle family)

the realization that my father will soon be making a similar journey. All those young soldiers boarding trains across the country. Will they survive? Will they come home maimed? I see them all as yellow ducks gliding across the back of the fairground booth—which ones will be shot without a thought—ping, ping, ping—and which ones will glide to safety? As my father said to me the one time I interviewed him about the war: "It was just the luck of the draw."

Auntie didn't know much more about how Fran died except that it happened on Okinawa and she thought he was hit in the shoulder and heart. If that's true, at least it would have been quick. What wasn't quick was how my father learned of his friend's death.

> May 17, 1945
> Dear Folks:
> Wrote to Fran and Bob today. Sure wish we could get together again.

In four days, Fran would be dead. But it would be two more months before my father was certain about his friend's fate.

> July 26, 1945
> Dear Folks:
> Have you heard any more about Fran yet?

Aug 17, 1945
Dear Folks:

I was sorry to hear about Fran. I kind of figured he was gone, but was hoping just the same. The telegram makes it official though. I wrote a letter to Fran's folks. It's a hard job to write a letter like that, but it had to be done.

September 9, 1945
Dear Folks:

I received a letter from Bob yesterday. The day he wrote the letter, he had just learned of Fran's death. He was pretty well broken up over it, and having a pretty hard time of it. He sounded pretty damned low in his letter.

I wonder what my father and mother would have told me about Fran if I had known to ask. Would I have learned more? Would they have opened up about such a bright flame being snuffed out prematurely? Or would they have just parroted the usual platitudes about the dead and changed the subject. My parents never offered much in the way of interior commentary, but based on the few occasions I directly asked them a difficult question, they would have been surprisingly open and perceptive. I sure wish I had known to ask.

CHAPTER 25

Coming Home

Bert had beat the odds. The mortality rate for B-17 airmen was 30 percent. The Fifteenth Air Force lost 1,850 bombers during the course of the war and of the original 646 combat personnel who arrived in Italy with his 483rd Bomb Group, 40 percent were either killed in action or became prisoners of war.

Bert survived the shrapnel wounds that earned him the Purple Heart and many near misses. He survived losing oxygen at 28,000 feet and dozens of thundering assaults by German flak guns and fighter planes. He survived the tainted Army food, a field dentist, and his mother's wrath for not writing more often. He avoided being blown up by their makeshift stove. He narrowly avoided a murderous late-night rock attack by hoodlums in a bombed-out Italian village. During training exercises in Florida, he was inches from being dropped 10,000 feet along with the practice bombs.

He regularly endured 10-hour missions at 50 degrees below zero and the privations of living in a muddy tent during a frigid Italian winter. He survived 24 sorties that were long enough and dangerous enough to count for 42 missions.

He survived to come home and marry Red. But not right away.

In the weeks after VE Day, Bert languished in Italy. He waited and waited, then waited some more to find out whether he would be reassigned to fight the Pacific war. On May 19, most of the crew, including Frank, was transferred to Pisa to serve as crew on transport planes shuttling discharged soldiers to North Africa to begin their flight home.

They had reached their minimum mission count and were reassigned to non-combat duty. But because Bert and three others didn't have the required number of missions, they stayed behind. Before he left, Frank painted the "Mr. Bones" logo on a new B-17 in memory of the plane they had arrived in.

> **May 20, 1945**
> Boys left for Pisa today. Sure hate to see them go. Took pictures of the boys and "Mr. Bones." Like leaving home.
>
> For a year, we had lived together, played together, and relied on each other. Parting was a wrenching experience. For many months, I tried to maintain the fiction that we would join up again in the States and head for the Pacific.
>
> **May 21, 1945**
> Moved over to Frank's corner. Kind of lonesome without the boys around.

Although Bert's reflections say little about the men he served with, there is one brief exception near the end of his manuscript. Again, he appears to be writing with Hemingway's iceberg theory in mind, and again, he leaves out so much the reader could easily miss the weight of emotion below the surface.

I don't know much about Frank Mullally, but I will share the few kernels of information that I have. My father and Frank stayed in touch throughout their long lives, but rarely saw each other after the war. The reason for their postage stamp friendship was that Frank joined a Franciscan monastery, became a priest, and spent the next half century as a missionary in the remote regions of Bolivia.

My brother was a foreign service officer in Bolivia for two years and had a chance to meet the legendary Frank. He stopped by the Franciscan church in La Paz soon after he arrived in the city and talked to the supervisory priest, but it took a long time for the message to reach Frank in whatever remote outpost he was living in at the time. One afternoon my brother got a call from an armed Marine corporal stationed at the embassy's bullet-proof guard station: "Some old guy who claims to be a priest says he's here see you," said the guard. When my brother walked into the lobby to meet his guest, he could see why the corporal was skeptical. Frank, who was in his seventies, looked more like a homeless person than a man of the cloth.

"He was wearing one of those old-style quilted jackets—the kind we wore before down became popular," my brother told me. "It was ripped in at least a dozen places and stitched back together with black thread. These guys take their vow of poverty seriously."

Frank practiced his vocation from the steaming jungles of the Amazon Basin to the soaring heights of the Andes. According to his obituary, "He spent many of his vacations walking for a week or more through isolated areas in the Bolivian countryside, celebrating the Eucharist, baptisms and marriages. It was common for him to walk long distances alone to give people the consolation of the sacrament."

Even before he made his Franciscan vow of poverty, Frank was a man of simple pleasures. When he was transferred with the bulk of the crew to Pisa, my father moved to Frank's corner of the tent at the Sterparone airfield.

> Living in Frank's corner brings to mind the saga of the pipe. To this day, all Frank ever wanted was a clean change of clothes, a pack of Bugler pipe tobacco, and his pipe. His cherished pipe was old—almost burnt through. The stem was held together with wire and tape. When he smoked, the pipe gurgled like a mud volcano and was as aromatic as an ill-kept locker room. Frank lost his beloved pipe but he and the instrument were so famous that a mechanic, dismantling an old B-17 discovered the pipe behind some armor plate. The mechanic tracked Frank down and he and his pipe were reunited.

★★★

For Bert, the end of the war meant more waiting, a skill honed during two and a half years in the Army. Finally, on June 8, a month after the war in Europe ended, Bert was granted a short furlough home before he was to be reassigned to the Pacific. Over the next four days, he hopscotched from Italy to Marrakesh, to the Azores, to Newfoundland, and finally to Bradley Field, just north of Hartford, Connecticut.

June 12, 1945
Flew from Newfoundland to Bradley Field. Even smelled different as we came across the border. This is wonderful. Processed this afternoon and evening. Miles Standish tomorrow. Talked on the phone to folks and Red. WHAT A DAY!

Because this was the Army, nothing was simple or efficient. He had traveled 8,000 miles over four days and had just landed 18 miles north of Hartford. But he still wasn't allowed to go home. After all, there was paperwork to deal with. So instead, the Army shipped him by train to two different Army bases and he spent four more days in "processing." On the first day of this bureaucratic torture, the train went right through Hartford and stopped for an hour in a rail yard less than a mile from his parents' home.

June 13, 1945
Went through Hartford yards. What a feeling. Should have jumped train.

Finally, on the fourth day of processing, his furlough was approved and his diary entry for that day was a single word:

June 16, 1945
HOME!

★★★

But "HOME!" didn't mean it was over. Although that was the last word in his retirement-age manuscript, it wasn't the end of his military service. This was not a discharge, and Bert was slated to resume bomber duty in the Pacific in support of the invasion of Japan, a dreaded mission that promised to be the bloodiest battles of the war. A week later, the overstretched elastic band known as an Army leave snapped back, yanking Bert away from Red and sling-shotting him to Sioux Falls, South Dakota, to prepare for the war in the Pacific.

July 24, 1945
Dear Bert:

Here we are beginning our correspondence again and I can't say that I like the idea much. Those days just seemed to fly by. A few of your old letters from Italy just arrived last night and you were wondering in them if my feelings towards you would change for the better. I guess you know that they have without my saying anything. Last night I thought about that time I just wouldn't let you leave me. It's a good thing we weren't alone because I might have whispered those three words in your ear. Many times I was tempted to. Honestly Bert, I don't know what keeps holding me back. Maybe the problem is that we try to live a lifetime of happiness in a few days. I'll be dreaming of you in a few minutes, so good night.

★★★

Bert never had to serve in the Pacific. President Truman canceled that assignment by dropping a pair of atomic bombs on Hiroshima and Nagasaki.

August 7, 1945
Dear Folks:

There's quite a bit of stir about the new bomb. It sure is a terrible thing. Perhaps it will end the war more quickly, and then it's up to the world to see that no one has a chance to use it again. God help all of us if there's ever another war though. We helped experiment with that stuff when we were in Italy. We used the first of the atomic fuses against an airfield in Germany last March. We only used the fuses however, and had no idea that they were making bombs too. It was quite hush-hush at the time.

In early August, news leaked of the Japanese surrender and many Americans jumped the gun, assuming the war was over when, in fact, it would be five days before Emperor Hirohito made his final decision.

Based on the false alarms, Mary Jane penned three celebratory letters in rapid succession.

> August 10, 1945
> Dear Bert:
> The news is so wonderful I can hardly believe it could happen. I haven't any idea where you are at this moment but the whole world knows now that the Japs have given up. Bert, our prayers are really answered now.... Tomorrow I start my vacation. I'll be thinking of you all the time when I'm at the beach. I'll just pretend you're with me when I go in swimming, when I'm lying on the beach, when I'm sitting on the rocks with all the gals. Oh Bert, imagine being home for good.

> August 13, 1945
> Dear Bert:
> Last night the sirens blew to announce the end of the war while we were over at Sound View. Everyone ran to the front of O'Connor's. Sailors and soldiers were kissing the dates, people were shouting and then the "Star Spangled Banner" began to play and everyone snapped to attention and began to sing with heart and souls. I got a lump in my throat and couldn't sing. I felt so happy and lonesome at the same time. I was wishing that the whole gang was there to celebrate. We didn't find out it was a false alarm until we hit Old Lyme Shores. What a letdown. You asked me to think of you often while I'm down here. Bert, I think of you all the time, regardless of where I am.

Then finally, after two false alarms, the Japanese Emperor addressed the world by radio and WWII was over at last.

> August 15, 1945
> Dear Bert:
> It's all over now. There was a lot of celebrating in Hartford. The streets were mobbed with people and traffic. In just about every paper I picked up today I saw pictures of servicemen kissing girls,

little children smiling, and waving flags, and crowds with their fingers formed in the victory V. In Sound View, Point of Woods and Niantic there was plenty of celebrating.

I still don't have any idea where you are but I know how happy you are. I can't believe that it's really over and soon all our friends will soon be home. It means that fathers will soon see their children, many of them for the first time. Fathers and mothers will see their sons and daughters who have been away for too long a time. Sweethearts will meet again, sisters will see brothers again, friends will meet again. At the same time, I can't help thinking of those who will never return. I felt so sorry for the loved one of these boys. On the other hand, they may be happier in Heaven than we can ever be here on earth. Everything would be complete if you were here to celebrate with me.

Of course, the Army couldn't just discharge these battle-weary soldiers now that the war was over. There still paperwork to fill out—mountains of it. So their release would take months rather than days. Though the war ended in August, Bert wasn't even sure if he'd be home in time for Christmas. The continued delays were excruciating for both Bert and Mary Jane after more than two years of courtship by mail.

August 20, 1945
Here I am writing on the couch in the sun parlor. The moon is shining beautifully on the water. What a beautiful night wasted! Why don't you jump in a plane and join me.... I always keep a letter on my stationery box so your address is always handy. The one that's there now is the one in which you asked about Bill. No Bert, I don't love Bill. Nothing will ever come of our former relationship. Let's just hope that you will be home soon and there won't be any need for me to write any more of my confusing, dopey letters.

CHAPTER 26

"Grazie di Cuore"

The letters continued until late November 1945 when Bert was finally discharged. He was home in time for Christmas and worked in a hammer factory for a while before he returned to Dartmouth, where he joined a fraternity and continued to date Mary Jane. I'm not quite sure how or when she finally decided to marry Bert, but my brother did tell me this story …

Soon after my father returned from the war, Mary Jane had several of the boys she dated over for dinner to welcome them home from overseas. These welcome-home dinners took place in rapid succession.

Mary Jane was still living with her parents and her favorite aunt was visiting from Manhattan. Auntie Dell had always taken a special interest in Mary Jane's well-being. From the time my mother was a little girl, Dell would have her down to her apartment in New York where she would lavish her favorite niece with attention and treat her to the sophisticated experiences of the big city.

I'm told that Dell was the smartest of the three Archer siblings, but by the time I knew her as Auntie Dell, she was a charming dingbat who told stories with great enthusiasm. Her blue eyes would widen with excitement as she told elaborate stories with "whosits" inserted for every person and "whatsits" for each thing. With no proper nouns, no one could follow who or what she was talking about. But we all laughed anyway because her enthusiasm was such a delight.

Whether she was like this in 1945, I can't say. I'm sure her word-retrieval skills were better, but I would imagine that her kookie persona was pretty much the same. As my brother tells it, Dell attended each of the welcome home dinners for Mary Jane's potential beaus. My father went first and Dell adored him. When Freddie Taylor came to dinner the next night, Dell turned to him partway through the meal and said, "Now Bert, tell me about …"

"No Auntie Dell, this is Freddie," said my mother.

"Oh dear," said Dell, putting her hand on the young man's arm. "I'm so sorry, Freddie." But ten minutes later, she was calling him Bert again. And she did the same thing to Bill Harney the following night, repeatedly calling him Bert throughout the evening.

I am certain that my batty great aunt knew exactly what she was doing. Her message to my mother was clear: "Bert is the one for you, dear." She was also sending a clear message to the other young men, by calling them all Bert.

In January 1948, my parents married and moved to Dartmouth together, where my mother got a job in the admissions office until my father graduated in 1950.

Dartmouth remained a paradise in my parents' memory—a New England village of incomparable beauty set among the foothills of the White Mountains, filled with bright young men, many of them returned from the war. It was an island of peace and tranquility where the biggest battle was the football game against Yale and the biggest danger was a C+. Dartmouth was a post-war idyll that nurtured a new marriage that lasted for the rest of their lives.

★★★

My parents were not exciting people. After Dartmouth, they were happy to plant their roots among the predictable green lawns of suburbia where they played couple's bridge and went to hospital parties. They raised two sons and joined the PTA. My father worked two jobs and played golf and poker with friends. They took the same vacation to the same place (Old Lyme Shores) in the same month each year, and went to the same restaurant every Friday night for three decades.

Ruins of the Mayan city of Palenque during our adventure in 1973. (The Ibelle family)

There were two shocking exceptions to their routine. In 1969, when I was a freshman in high school, they pulled us out of school for three weeks in February so the four of us could explore archeological sites from Mexico City to the Guatemala border.

It was radical. It was an adventure. They were even breaking the rules by taking us out of school for several weeks to explore the present and ancient culture of Mexico. We traipsed through the ruins of the Toltec, Aztec, Mixtec, Olmec, Zapotec, and Mayan civilizations, then finished it off with five days on the beach at Acapulco. Nobody in my town did shit like that. It changed my life. I wanted more.

They surprised me a second time the year after I went off to college. My father, the man who spent his adult life working and reading, responded to the empty nest by earning his pilot's license and buying a plane. My god, the man on the couch just bought a freaking airplane! I couldn't believe it. On weekends my parents flew to airstrips all across

Bert and Mary Jane loved to fly over the family cottage and then out to the islands for breakfast. (The Ibelle family)

New England together, but their favorite trip was to fly down the Connecticut River to the coast, circle the cottage a few times, then continue east to one of the islands—Nantucket, Martha's Vineyard, or Block. They'd land on the island in time for lunch, walk around the village for a while, then head home so they were back at their dining room table in South Windsor in time for dinner. They never took their plane on an extended trip or even stayed overnight. They had stepped out of their routine in a big way. But they were still creatures of habit.

A few years later, they went on a three-week trip to Italy. It was the first time my father had been back since the war and they fell in love with the country. It was so different from the squalid Italy my father described in a 1945 letter home to his parents. The Italy they experienced in the 1970s was a country of incomparable beauty, filled with the world's finest art and people who knew how to live life to its fullest.

The trip had a fitting climax when they visited the island of Capri, where my father spent his one furlough during the war. One evening,

Bert and Mary Jane during their retirement in Old Lyme. (The Ibelle family)

while they were dining at an outdoor restaurant overlooking the harbor 700 feet below, they noticed a well-dressed Italian gentleman at a nearby table who kept glancing over at them. When the gentleman finished his meal, he got up and stepped over to my parents' table and said, "You were here during the war, yes?" When my father confirmed the conjecture, the gentleman took my father's hand in his and said, "*Grazie di cuore* [thank you with all my heart]," bowed, and continued on his way. A minute later, a waiter came to their table with a bottle of fine red wine, compliments of the Italian gentleman.

★★★

I first conceived of this book as a way to make World War II come alive for readers by telling the story of three people who lived it—one in Europe, one in the Pacific, and one at home. I wanted to put you in their place so that you could see and feel the war rather than consider it from a distance as part of the grand sweep of history.

It wasn't long before I realized that this project was also a search for my father, an elusive man who I have known since birth, yet never fully knew. In this sense, it's a universal story—for who among us has not yearned to know their parents when they were still young and excited by the possibilities of life?

Now, as my search nears its conclusion, I realize that this book is, at its core, a love letter to my parents. I hope you have come to love them too.

CHAPTER 27

Journey's End

I first read my father's retirement-age war memoir hoping it would provide a window into my old man's soul. It did not. I was baffled by the lack of introspection about war, love, and friendship. I planned to use my interviewing skills to gently coax him beyond the facts. But like so many things in life, I never got around to it.

There are hundreds of questions I would like to ask the two of them to fill in the holes. But they are gone, as are all the people who knew them during that period.

When I think of my parents these days, the world seems a bit lonely. How can two people who have always been in my life, be so completely and utterly gone? It's been ten years now and still, whenever my wife and I do something exciting—or even mildly interesting—I catch myself thinking, "I'll call Mom. She'll love this ... oh wait ..."

Growing up, I was disappointed by my parents' aversion to adventure, but maybe I made the error of judging them by my own values, which is unfair since they never judged me by theirs. So why has it taken me so long to cut them the same slack they granted me from birth?

When my father returned home from the war at the end of 1945 he already had all the adventure he needed for a lifetime. Near the end of his career, when he relearned how to fly and bought that plane, he had no interest in a grand adventure. He was satisfied with a far more rewarding journey: flying to breakfast on Nantucket with his wife of four decades. After all, wasn't it a life with Red that he yearned for all

My mother and I when I was a junior in high school. (The Ibelle family)

those years before when he flew over the Alps at age 20 on his way to possible oblivion?

Although my father's interior life remains elusive, I did find him in a way. In that box of letters and his retirement journal, I found a young man in love, struggling with the profound loneliness of a forced separation from everyone he held dear. I witnessed the gleeful sense of adventure of a college freshman as he hopscotched across three continents on his way to the war. And I found a young man who had to do terrifying, horrible things, while living and fighting in some of the worst conditions imaginable. I'm perplexed by his lack of any mixed feelings about dropping 5,000 pounds of explosives on factories and railyards, knowing that many of those bombs would miss their targets and hit the homes and workplaces of civilians. But it was a different time, and I have never been to war, so maybe it's not possible for me to understand.

My generation's outrage over Vietnam must have felt like a rebuke to Bert and 16 million others—men conscripted to do brutal things to save the world from even more brutal things. So when I tried to probe this issue in that phone call to my father after I flew in a B-17, he replied in typical Bert Ibelle fashion:

"It was the business we were in."

Bert in Old Lyme with his two sons. (Left) the author, (right) his brother Bob. (The Ibelle family)

Hemingway's iceberg. Its shimmering tip was floating in front of me and there was no way to reach the frozen mass of emotions that lay beneath the surface.

I deeply regret my failure to interview my father about the war. But even if I had, I probably would have run face-first into the wall he had built to seal off the two years he spent as an indentured servant in Hell. It was a role he would never examine or even admit to. Why would he? He had built a wall around those feelings so he could come home and be the husband, father, friend, and scholar he was meant to be.

My father was fortunate that WWII was one of the rare instances when the massive sin of war actually did some good. They defeated Hitler and that was all the justification he needed. So his generation left the introspection and moral hand-wringing to their offspring—kids who could avoid the devil's bargain simply by writing a few college papers while consuming massive quantities of beer. The college-bound members of my generation have been able to look war in the eye because we never had to touch it.

APPENDIX I

Mission List

#	Date	Target		Pilot	Sorties	Missions
1	Dec. 25, 1944	Brux, Czechoslovakia	Synthetic oil refinery	Frink	1	2
2	Dec. 28, 1944	Regensburg, Germany	Marshalling yards	Frink	1	2
3	Jan. 4, 1945	Verona, Italy	Marshalling yards	Frink	1	1
4	Jan. 21, 1945	Vienna, Austria	Oil refinery	Frink	1	2
5	Feb. 7, 1945	Vienna, Austria	Schwechat oil refinery	Frink	1	2
6	Feb. 15, 1945	Vienna, Austria	Supply depot	Frink	1	2
7	Feb. 17, 1945	Linz, Austria	Benzine plant	Frink	1	2
8	Feb. 20, 1945	Vienna, Austria	Schwechat oil refinery	Frink	1	2

(Continued)

#	Date	Target		Pilot	Sorties	Missions
9	Feb. 21, 1945	Vienna, Austria	Goods depot	Frink	1	2
10	Feb. 27, 1945	Augsburg, Germany	Marshalling yards	Frink	1	2
11	Mar. 2, 1945	Linz, Austria	Marshalling yards	Frink	1	2
12	Mar. 8, 1945	Hegyeshalom, Hungary	Marshalling yards	Frink	1	2
13	Mar. 13, 1945	Regensburg, Germany	Marshalling yards	Frink	1	2
14	Mar. 16, 1945	Weiner Neustadt, Austria	Marshalling yards	Frink	1	2
15	Mar. 20, 1945	Vienna (Kagran), Austria	Oil refineries	Frink	1	2
16	Mar. 22, 1945	Ruhland, Germany	Oil refineries	Frink	1	2
17	Mar. 25, 1945	Prague, Poland	Kbely Airport	Frink	1	2
18	Apr. 2, 1945	Graz, Austria	Marshalling yards	Frink	1	2
19	Apr. 6, 1945	Verona, Italy	RR bridge	Frink	1	1

#	Date	Target		Pilot	Sorties	Missions
20	Apr. 17, 1945	Bologna, Italy	Command post	Frink	1	1
21	Apr. 18, 1945	Bologna, Italy	Front lines	Gammin	1	1
22	Apr. 20, 1945	Fortezza, Italy	Marshalling yards	Foster	1	1
23	Apr. 24, 1945	Autraburg, Germany	RR bridge	Frink	1	2
24	Apr. 26, 1945	Bolzano, Italy	Ammo dump	Anderson	1	1
Total					**24**	**42**

APPENDIX II

The Crew of the "Mr. Bones"

Standing (left to right): Alvin "Casey" Stengle, ball turret, Palo Alto, California; Frank Mullally, radio, Union City, New Jersey; Ben Lambert, tail gunner, Conway, Pennsylvania; Lou Morehouse, top turret, Memphis, Tennessee; Gene Wisby, left waist gunner, Stockton, California; Bert Ibelle, right waist gunner, Hartford, Connecticut. Kneeling (left to right): Bob Foulis, co-pilot, Kenmore, New York; Ted Frink, pilot, North Haverhill, New Hampshire; Dick Swears, navigator, Kansas City, Kansas. (The Ibelle family)